LOVE
THE HOUSE
YOU'RE IN

LOVE THE HOUSE YOU'RE IN

Paige Rien

40 WAYS

TO IMPROVE YOUR
HOME AND CHANGE
YOUR LIFE

BOULDER
2016

Roost Books
An imprint of Shambhala Publications, Inc.
4720 Walnut Street
Boulder, Colorado 80301
roostbooks.com

First Edition
Printed in the United States of America

♾This edition is printed on acid-free paper that meets the American
National Standards Institute Z39.48 Standard.
♻Shambhala Publications makes every effort to print on recycled
paper. For more information please visit www.shambhala.com.

Distributed in the United States by Penguin Random House LLC
and in Canada by Random House of Canada Ltd

Illustrations by Claudia Pearson
Designed by Danielle Deschenes

Library of Congress Cataloging-in-Publication Data

Rien, Paige.
Love the house you're in: 40 ways to improve your home and change
your life / Paige Rien.—First edition.
pages   cm
Includes index.
ISBN 978-1-61180-198-9 (pbk.: acid-free paper)
1. House furnishings. 2. Interior decoration. 3. Dwellings—Remodeling.
I. Title.
TX311.R54 2015
645—dc23
2015008352

645 RIE
 1821 8449 03-09-2016 BLP
Rien, Paige,

Love the house you're in
            KHP

FOR FRANCIS

Home is the nicest
word there is.

—LAURA INGALLS WILDER

CONTENTS

INTRODUCTION

I know what you're going to say. You just don't love your house. You bought it because of the schools or the yard or the price, but you come home after a long day and think, Yuck. *You wish it were different. Badly. You need it to be different—to look better, to work better, and to make you feel better. I've been there many times myself.*

If you want to love your house, here's the secret: it doesn't come from a really great couch or the perfect happiness-inducing paint color. It doesn't spring forth from the best interior designer or reading the most popular design blogs. *It comes from within you.* It comes when you fearlessly put yourself into your home and tell your life story throughout. It comes when you stop looking at what everyone else is doing. It comes not when everything matches but when the spaces match *you* and what you're all about.

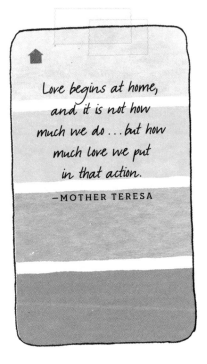

Love begins at home, and it is not how much we do . . . but how much love we put in that action.

—MOTHER TERESA

MY STORY AND THE REASON FOR THIS BOOK

My husband, Francis, and I have lived in lots of fixer-uppers together, and we've made homes out of all of them by doing almost everything together, (mostly) harmoniously. As we were renovating a giant three-story seaside house from the 1890s (a task that required us to wear winter coats to bed for two months and taxed our relationship in ways I don't care to revisit), I was hired to be a designer for HGTV's very popular show *Hidden Potential* for five seasons. While the "glamour" of television was fun, I began to miss getting my hands dirty and, most important, I missed the design process. Television compresses the journey I find so interesting—the collaboration and construction needed to go from idea to new space—and perpetuates some big design myths. Big change doesn't happen, nor should it happen, overnight or while you were out. And unfortunately, television designers don't have all the answers.

E-mails from frustrated, desperate, even despondent viewers inspired this book. Despite an ocean of ideas, options, and inspiring images from TV, blogs, Pinterest, Houzz, and countless shelter magazines, many home owners remain lost or disenchanted with home improvement. What we have collectively forgotten in the blizzard of leather poufs, reclaimed wood tables, and ubiquitous ikat is that to make a home great, we need to spend less time in the marketplace and more time with ourselves.

Looking outward all the time—at things in stores, at other people's houses—or always listening to what people like me have to say disconnects us from what we really need and want. The result is a lot of unhappiness. It's easy to get lost in too many options, with unworkable ideas and questionable advice. If you feel defeated, congratulations: you are hereby motivated to make your house better, and you are the reason for this book.

HOW DO YOU START?

This is not a typical interior design book. There is not one picture of my work or my house in these pages. There is no eye candy, there are no big reveals or design secrets. Here is what you'll find instead:

A process based on self-reflection and self-knowledge. I ask a lot of questions. First the all-important ones: *Who am I? What's my story?* Then house-specific ones: *What feeling do I want for this room?* Ultimately, it's "Your Turn" at the end of each chapter to apply what you know of yourself to your home. In the end, even if you do hire an architect, a designer, or a decorator to help you (and I don't advocate for or against the practice), the work you do with this book will help you get the most out of that relationship.

A fresh perspective and approach. Begin to see your house as sacred and the work on it as art. Where we lay our heads, teach our children, heal and rejuvenate ourselves, and experience the ups and downs of modern life is truly sacred ground. The process is intensely creative, the outcome deeply personal and expressive. Compose your house like an artist, taking your time, going your own way, and finding the joy in the process.

Strategies for creating a home that works for your lifestyle and personality. Go beyond looks and thoughtfully consider the feeling you are trying to create in your house. Homes are capable of doing many important things: calming us, centering us, inspiring us. They can also tell an honest and engaging narrative about us. Make your home fabulous for you and beautifully about you, and it will become an interesting place for whomever visits.

Simple tools and ideas for making your story shine throughout your home. Put your ideas about "style" away for a bit. The word *style* is vague and overused by retailers to sell you more things. Instead, think of your *story* and those things that really matter to you and have shaped you as your guide. When you do this, you'll find that your home likely defies any one style category.

Encouragement and confidence-boosting advice. I challenge you to trust yourself. We're taught to think others have better taste or creative abilities than we do. For something as intimate as your home, you are by far the best person for the job. What you need to make your house great is not money, time, or advice, but confidence. You'll be encouraged to rebuff influences that stifle you from bringing yourself into your home. Making your home yours is a job made for you, whether you believe it now or not.

My hope is that when you look within yourself for homemaking answers, the process is dramatically easier and the end result much more satisfying (and long-lasting).

There are five sections in this book. The first section is 100 percent introspective—asking you to stop and put yourself in focus. The second section invites you to gain a greater understanding of your home so you know what you're working with. The third section steps out of cerebral work and into the design process, encouraging you to consider applying all you've learned, setting the tone in your home for the story you want to tell. The fourth section moves through each room so you can consider how it is used and how to create a house that functions well for you. Finally, the fifth section discusses the process of curating for your home and filling it with things you're connected to. I suggest starting with Part One, but after that feel free to skip around however you like or according to what your home needs. Let's do this!

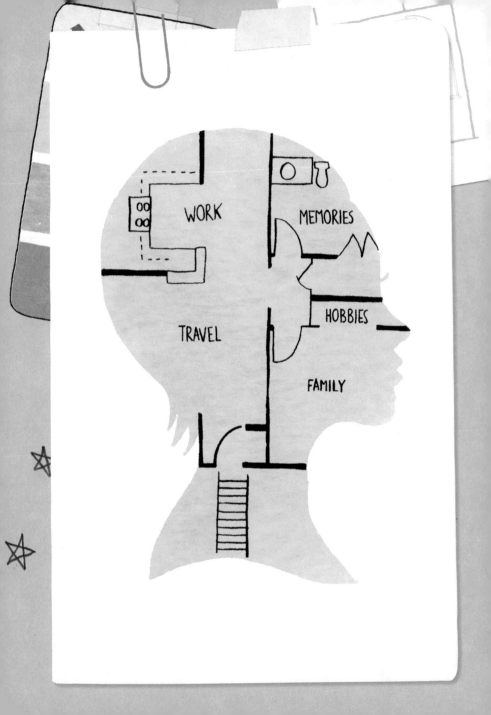

Part One

SO, WHO ARE YOU?

We can't jump into drapes or paint chips just yet. Before you can make great, lasting, physical changes to your home, you first need a solid foundation of understanding and clarity. Keep an open mind. Contrary to what we're told in commercials such as, "More saving, more doing" (Home Depot's tagline), the tools here involve thinking, dreaming, and writing. These are the tools for getting unstuck.

When your life and your story form the taproot for the look and feel of your home, it becomes a living, breathing entity that will grow and evolve with you. In this section, we gather the essentials—the components of your life that will later help fill in those blanks to questions like, *What colors should I choose? Do I need a formal dining room?* This section will have you digging for the answers that will give you the clarity and confidence to trust yourself as you move forward.

1

START BY STOPPING

You're officially in process! Take a break from buying anything, soliciting any advice, or making any decisions for now. Instead, collect thoughts, photos, and notes for this journey of house-making.

Making a beautiful home is within your grasp. Yes, you can do it—all by your lonesome, if need be, and with what you've got in your bank account. For now, you don't need any magazines, blogs, or pros in your corner. You don't need more money or more time, but you will need patience and faith in yourself and your house.

Start by taking a big, deep breath and being open to a new way of change. If you are knee-deep in a Pinterest-Houzz-magazine-HGTV blizzard of "inspirational" photos, designer tips, and ideas from elsewhere, put it all away. Remember that scene in *Star Wars* when Obi-Wan Kenobi tells Luke Skywalker to close his eyes and trust the Force? It's a bit like that. Look inward first; the answers are there, not where you've been searching.

First, stop spending money. There will be plenty of time to buy, make, or otherwise acquire new things. For now, put away your credit cards. Even if you have a straightforward problem, such as needing a hamper, wait. Don't buy your way out just yet.

I'd rather you have a pile of laundry on the floor than buy even a small item you'll hate six months from now.

Here's the thing: just buying more stuff won't get you the house you love. Our tastes change and are often manipulated by the tsunami of commercial messages, images, and things being sold to us each and every moment of our lives. What we like may be different based on whether we are hungry, have heard upsetting news that day, or have smelled wafts of chocolate in a retail environment. Remember, once we spend our money on something for our house, we've created the expectation that this purchase will improve things. If it truly does, well done. If it doesn't (and that's a lot of pressure to put on a throw pillow), we feel disappointed, as if we've wasted our money. This book is about helping you feel better, not making you feel worse.

It's time to be pickier and harder to please. Get clear on what a house that reflects you looks like. Wait, do a bit of legwork, find clarity, and when you finally do buy (if you still need to), the results will be different. You won't hope that what you buy will work—you'll know it will.

Second, stop asking anyone else for help for now. There is nothing wrong with either free or paid design help, but right now it's premature. Before someone else can help you, you must get clear on who you are and what you really want in your home. If you were to hire a design professional without being clear on your desires for your home and exactly who you are, it would not be good for either of you. So don't ask your mother what she thinks of the drapes. Don't ask your neighbor if you should paint your front door. Go inward for the moment. Democracy is suspended, and monarchy is restored. You're the king or queen, and everyone else is fired, or at least on furlough.

Third, take a vacation from all your favorite house-themed websites and publications. Go on a Pinterest diet, ditch Houzz for a while, and leave all those busy design bloggers be for a bit. While the wealth of information, ideas, advice, inspiring photos, and online messages is wonderful and has radically changed home improvement for all of us, it is useful to turn it off every so often. If you are unhappy in your house and unsure where to go, this is your moment to turn it all off. A flood of messages of easy projects, simple updates, DIY refreshes, and other things being done by others, seemingly with a snap of their fingers, is not helpful. Try looking inward instead of online. Not forever, but for now. Not for everything, just everything house-related.

> *Wherever you are is always the right place. There is never a need to fix anything, to hitch up the bootstraps of the soul and start at some higher place. Start right where you are.*
>
> **—JULIA CAMERON**

While on your media diet, start a Home Book. This will be a repository for all your notes, measurements, buying options, introspection, pictures, and dreams. You may already have a dream file, a collection of images from magazines, or a Pinterest board full of pictures you've found online. The House Book is like a 3-D dream house file with more depth. You will need more than just a file folder, and it cannot be done digitally. You need to be able to write in it and stick things like paint chips, fabric swatches, and business cards in it with ease.

Most clients are happy to supply me with piles of magazine photos they've collected over time. Collecting images that appeal to you is not an effective tool on its own. For one thing, there is no connection between image and execution—after you clip the picture of the phenomenal house in Malibu, how or what do you transfer to your home in Missoula? And when you create a dream file of images from *Architectural Digest* or the Pottery Barn catalog, you're limiting yourself to rooms designed by someone else for someone else's life. You may like the life displayed in an *Architectural Digest* spread, but trust that your own life is the best backdrop for your home. Homes are like fingerprints.

Rather than just a dream file, our Home Book will also act as a journal. It may seem odd to get a journal assignment in a book on home improvement/design, but much comes from personal writing in any creative process, especially such an intimate one. This has been overlooked in design media. Sure, ours is a visual business, built on color and material selection and composition. We're also working in emotional and deeply personal territory. The answers to making a home that reflects the best of you is within you.

Your Home Book will have pictures from other people's homes, but it will also have pictures of your home. It will show features you like, aspects you hate, and spaces you're working on. Don't underestimate how differently you will see your own house in photographs. Your Home Book is home, so to speak, for anything and everything that has to do with your house. You might be thinking, *Is there an app for that?* There may be, but unless you're building a life online, the bits and pieces that go into home-building must be tangible and remain touchable.

1   Get a notebook that will be your Home Book. A thick, hardbound, 8½ × 11-inch notebook is ideal.

2   On the cover or first page of your Home Book, paste a picture of some part of your home that you like. It can be a photo of the front of your house with flowers blooming, your favorite corner, your Christmas tree, a view from a window—it doesn't matter. Choose a picture that features something you like, even if it's a small detail.

3   Keep your Home Book on hand as you work through this book and as you work on your home—and whenever you go to shop or seek inspiration.

Design is an opportunity
to continue telling
the story, not just to sum
everything up.
—TATE LINDEN

2

WHAT'S YOUR STORY?

*Zero in on your own personal narrative
and tell it throughout your home.*

All too often the answer to a design problem is simply to find a set of products that all share the same "style" and fill your house with them. This is a formula, and interesting spaces with soul don't follow formulas. *Style* is the most overused word in home design. Can any single style describe the whole that is you and what you need, love, and want to express in your home? No. Style also encourages you to ally with a particular aesthetic and show it throughout your house, as opposed to telling a story with the many pieces of your life and composing them in an elegant way. This is how you create a personal home: you defy category.

When we're asked, "What's your style?" in regard to our homes, we're meant to give one of three one-word options with a few variants—*modern, traditional,* and *transitional* are the favorites, often followed by *eclectic, bohemian,* and *country.* The question really asks you to reduce yourself to a word so that you can easily be accommodated with a store, a catalog, or a search on a furniture website. These one-word categories represent such vastness in terms of what can possibly be included in each that it's absurd to use them at all. Don't get me started on how the word *modern* is misused and how often. Don't be limited to one word when describing the art that is your home.

Rather than your style, consider the long, varied, and colorful history of your life. Your history is composed of a vast array of experiences—some positive, some negative. It's your heritage, your journey before and after your partner, before and after your children, likely in several different homes. Your story includes all your travel, your education, your faith, your accomplishments, and your life's transitions. It includes hardships and loss, disappointments and frustrations you've worked through. Consider also where you're going and what you want for your future.

Beware of telling someone else's story. So much decor sold today through catalogs and home goods stores have faux stories. Plaster placards with French sayings from an imaginary Parisian restaurant, withered birdhouses, factory-aged nautical knots in frames whose maritime experience is limited to the inside of a container ship from China. There isn't anything wrong with these decorations, often conveniently priced for disposability when they are no longer in fashion. However, these items, like countless others, are meant to tell a story. But whose story exactly? If an item doesn't have anything to do with you, you're buying someone else's idea, someone else's opinion, and creating a space that is disconnected from your heart and who you are. That's not the route to creating a home you love and that loves you back. Mine your own story first, and start with what's true about you. This will radically change how and why you shop for your home.

I grew up in New Jersey. It's a part of my story that I choose not to curate throughout the house, especially since at this point, I've lived in many other places. However, going to the Jersey Shore was a huge part of my upbringing and has become a new tradition with my own kids. In my bathroom, there are three framed vintage

Jersey Shore postcards. I love them. They are my bits and pieces of New Jersey, my Jersey Shore, if you will.

You don't need to make your story obvious to others, but what you use should be pleasing to *your* eye, inspire nostalgia, create a positive connection to memories, or better yet, all three of those things.

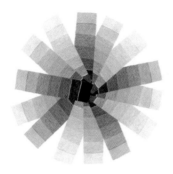

1   *What five adjectives describe you? Don't overthink this. Ready, go!*

2   *If you were stranded on a desert island, what five things would you not want to live without?*

3   *What have been the three best days of your life? Again, don't overthink it. What comes to mind first?*

4   *What gives you joy in your everyday life?*

5   *Are the answers to questions 1–4 told in your house? If not, why?*

3

WHERE HAVE YOU CALLED HOME?

*Look back at the experiences you
had in your childhood home, and in all
your previous residences, to understand
your definition of home.*

Where did you start? Like our respective childhoods, some of us
are trying to re-create the family homes in which we grew up; others
aim to fashion homes that are very different from where they were
raised. It's helpful to consider your first home, your life as a child,
vacations with your parents, and your first years in school. What did
all these environments look like?

Many people regard the homes they grew up in as "dated" or
"old-fashioned." If you generally had a positive experience growing
up and you remember your home as a nurturing space where you
felt love, include something from this first home in your current
one. The narrative you are telling in your home starts way back
when, with your childhood. There is more than nostalgic charm
in having things from your early years in your current home;
connections to childhood feel good and connect us to our youth.

Think about the house you grew up in. What did you like
about it? It doesn't matter if it's now considered horribly outdated.
Was there anything in the house that felt good? Was there
something you'd like to continue in your own home? Think about

> I believe that one can never leave home. I believe that one carries the shadows, the dreams, the fears and the dragons of home under one's skin, at the extreme corners of one's eyes and possibly in the gristle of the earlobe.
>
> —MAYA ANGELOU

how your house was organized spatially. Most homes built in the 1960s or before were not as open as they are today. Builders and architects back then created independent spaces for cooking, dining, and living for people with fewer things. Today, homes are either opened up through renovation or built new with an "open kitchen" as a prerequisite. What worked about the house you grew up in? What didn't? Think about your past spaces functionally and aesthetically. Once you've considered the home or homes in which you were raised, consider the other homes you visited often. What memories do you have of your grandmother's house? A neighbor's house?

This isn't necessarily about hand-me-downs, although things passed down through generations may do the job of connecting you to your childhood home. This is more about symbolism. My mother, like many in the early 1980s, went through a country phase when I was growing up. Like so many other things that fit into a style box, she got tired of it, someone decided it was no longer in vogue, or both. To this day, the hearts and pineapples of that faux-country aesthetic make me wince a bit. But I do love things of a bygone era, and the seeds of this were probably planted while looking at all those wooden apples and Early American decorative items in my childhood home.

My aunt had a painting of a little girl that hung over her bed. I can remember sleeping over at her house and admiring it, especially when she let me try on her dresserful of costume jewelry for hours at a time. I had always assumed the painting was a portrait of my aunt. After she died, I discovered the painting was by Renoir—and from a magazine. This "painting" that conjures such beautiful childhood memories for me and that now makes me laugh hangs in my foyer.

Perhaps there are no "artifacts" from your past that you want to insert directly into your spaces, but there is a lesson or a sensibility you can mimic. My grandmother's house overflowed with her handicrafts. Despite having three daughters and a husband deployed at war for four years, she tirelessly created things for her home. She was a master seamstress, and nearly everything that could be was adorned with ruffles, ball fringe, tassels, or some other kind of trim. She rotated her colorful and textured tissue boxes, handmade wreaths, and curtains seasonally; her prolific creativity would make even the busiest Etsy contributor feel lazy. What I loved was that she was everywhere in her house—I saw her work and her hands on everything. And if I didn't see it, I smelled it. Her house always smelled of her delectable homemade tomato sauce—something I've tried to mimic in my own home with little success. She was most certainly not going for a certain style.

I loved seeing the same chintz patterns in curtains, skirts, pillow trim, quilts, even wreaths. I can barely sew a button, but her handiwork made an impression on me. I believe I carry my grandmother's spirit into my house, even if I don't make fabric covers for my tissue boxes. She taught me to make my house fabulous, according to me, with whatever I've got.

It's worth taking a look at the homes in which you grew up, and perhaps the homes you've had as an adult, leading up to the home you're in now. Your past experiences in other kinds of spaces, perhaps in other climates or environments, prepare you for the kind of home owner you are today. Consider what worked, what didn't, and what you've learned. Consider what you'd like to see again in your current space and what you definitely do not want. It's all usable!

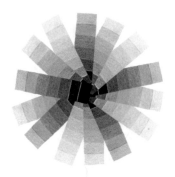

1 List five attributes or short phrases that describe the house you grew up in.

2 Think about a house other than your own in which you had a lot of good times. In five words, what made it awesome?

3 Name two things you loved about your childhood home itself, or the home from question 2, that you'd like to re-create in your own house.

4 What makes you feel like you're "home"? (List five words or short phrases.)

5 Do you have this feeling in your own home today? If not, why?

Our heritage and ideals,
our code and standards—
the things we live by and
teach our children—are
preserved or diminished by
how freely we exchange
ideas and feelings.

—WALT DISNEY

4

WHAT ARE YOUR ROOTS?

*Connect to your roots and consider
your heritage as a wellspring for
design inspiration.*

Rarely are we encouraged by design media to include our ethnic heritage in our home's aesthetic. As in matters of belief and religion, perhaps it's just too specific to show a home awash in the pride of one's heritage beyond generic Americana. This is a shame, considering we or our forebears all come from wildly, randomly, exquisitely different places. It's ironic that we live in such a diverse country, and yet what is most fashionable—if you look at the major catalogs and retailers—is a watered-down, nondescript, European aesthetic.

The homes of my relatives are awash in ethnic pride. I grew up looking at Greek pottery and Orthodox icons with their gaunt faces on the walls of my Aunt Paula's house. On tabletops my grandmother alternated between embroidered tablecloths from Hungary in bold reds, greens, purples, and black (subdued they are not) and the ethereal hand-sewn white lace from her mother that looked like it was about to dissolve into nothing. These things told our family's story. Heritage is the foundation of our identity. Homes with identity have soul.

When considering what story to tell in your home, it's worth looking at your people and where they came from—whether it's the

Mayflower in the early 1600s or Santo Domingo two years ago. It's worth expressing your ties to those who came before you. For me, this is Italy, but it's also New Jersey and Philadelphia, where I spent a lot of time growing up. It's Hungary, which I've visited twice, and Greece and Albania, which I've yet to visit but still feel strangely familiar. This is not so much about adopting the aesthetic of the country of your ancestors as it is about connecting your present home with them in some way. This can be done with books, art, heirlooms, or even ways of living.

My dear friend Wanda grew up in Mississippi, but she has lived in lots of other cities since and even more houses. She describes what she calls "working toward finding that Southern soul" wherever she lives. She is tenacious in finding it, bringing a bit of Mississippi and a bit of Georgia into many other regions of the country. Her homes are colorful, elaborate, and formal. Nothing is blah. Each house is quickly set up to entertain an army with crystal. Wanda draws on homes and experiences of her childhood, as well as the homes of family members still in Mississippi whom she misses dearly. Bring your roots with you wherever you go; they keep you company.

What journeys, within the United States perhaps, did your parents or grandparents make? There is something powerful in using maps that help tell your story or that of your relatives—to visitors or your children, or as a reminder to yourself. Better yet, use maps you've actually used in your travels. The wonder and beauty of the journey, so much a part of the immigrant experience, as well as the experience of people who have just moved around a lot, is worth displaying.

Think about what roots deserve a spot in your house.

1   Where did you grow up? What part of the local flora, architecture, food, or music was a big part of your life? How can you bring some of this into your space?

2   What ethnic heritage was dominant for you growing up? What are the colors, smells, foods, and images from this heritage? Can they be worked into your linens, paint colors, pillows, artwork, serveware?

3   Do you have items in your home that remind you of your cultural heritage? Why or why not? If you love something connected to your cultural heritage, but you're not sure how to use it or where to put it, first note its features—color, shape, scale, masculinity/femininity—and then let it "live" in different spaces in your home until one feels right.

Paris is always a good idea.
—AUDREY HEPBURN

5

WHERE HAVE YOU TRAVELED?

Use your life's travel experiences,
near and far, as fodder for great
design decisions.

Most of us hope to see more of the world. Some are fortunate
enough to have well-worn passports and stories from many foreign
countries or tales from multiple cross-country road trips in the US.
Travel shapes us the same way other forces, such as our education,
faith, upbringing, and hobbies, shape us. Travel stays with us
because of the feelings we had on whatever journey we took, so it's
worth borrowing from the places we've enjoyed the most.

How do you translate a lifetime of travel experiences into
your home? There is no one way. It starts with thinking about the
strongest memories you have of past experiences. Think about
the places that shaped your life well after you returned home.
Find a way to get those unforgettable places into your house. Go
beyond framed photos of your journey and bric-a-brac picked
up on your way. There is nothing wrong with the things you buy
or the pictures you've taken, but consider other reminders. My
husband and I were fortunate enough to go to French Polynesia
for our honeymoon. The week was a bit of a blur, but I have a large
pink shell, clearly not from the Jersey Shore, that I keep out on my
bookshelf. It's a hearty specimen, intact after nearly ten moves and

four children, and it reminds me of our honeymoon—the sweetness, the exoticness, the extraordinary physical beauty. I have a hundred photos in a box somewhere, but keeping the shell out is easier, less obvious, and really just for me. Infusing your space with your personal travel experiences is not for anyone else's benefit. It's not to show off or tell anyone where you've been—it's to infuse where you live with the feelings, emotions, and rich memories of travel. This is most powerfully done without pictures.

Often, we have little to show for our trips. In those cases, connect new purchases to experiences that left impressions on you. Use travel to remind you of lifestyles you appreciated or were in awe of. Think about how you felt. Think about the different ways people lived. When I visited distant relatives in Hungary, the hospitality I experienced there touched me in a way few experiences have; I have never been greeted with such unabashed festivity, generosity, and love from people I was meeting for the first time. Some of our meals were staged on long tables in living rooms, others were moved outside, most were enjoyed while our hosts stood behind us, ecstatic just to watch us eat. This athletic approach to the big family meal, with an always endless array of delicacies in quantities well beyond thrice what was necessary, had an impact on the kind of host I am, the kind of kitchen I've designed for myself, and the kind of expandable dining room I want some day.

What if you haven't traveled much? What if you plan to travel in the future, when your children or bank accounts are bigger? Part of your home should remind you of where you long to visit. Remember, a personal home includes where we've been, who we are now, where we are going, and who we hope to be. If you've never been to Italy but like the idea, by all means, invite Italy into your house. But think about what parts of Italy you're drawn to. Consider what you're likely to see and experience. Don't just buy American-knickknack-styled Italy. Research the kind of trip you'd like to take in travel magazines, books, and videos. Take the real trip, for sure, if you possibly can, but in the meantime, do the homework about what you're personally drawn to about a place and add the place to your space based on that.

Don't tell me how educated you are, tell me how much you have traveled.

—MOHAMMED

Even travel that happened without you can color your home. My husband brought two large plates, awash in a strange mix of blues, oranges, and turquoise, from Turkey into our relationship. We did not do this trip together, and for years, those plates lived in a box. Then a spot in our house appeared, begging for something blue, interesting, and with a story. The plates now flank a window I can see from my front yard as I drive up. I love that they remind me of Francis before we met, doing his own aimless travel in a part of the world I've yet to see. If you have stuff from your travels, but don't have an obvious place for it, hang on to it. If you have an organized design arsenal, you'll be able to shop in your own house sometime in the future. If it has story value, you'll find a place for it one day.

1 *Close your eyes. What's your strongest travel memory? What are the colors around you? What's the temperature? What do you smell, taste, and hear? Be specific. Linger in your memory.*

2 *Can you use a color, texture, shape, pattern, scent, or sound from your answer to question 1 as inspiration for a room in your house?*

3 *Think about one simple lifestyle difference in a place you've visited that you might like to adopt as your own—such as afternoon tea, late-night family dinners, chopsticks. These cultural differences may lead to shifts in your aesthetic as well.*

6

WHAT IS YOUR FAITH?

*Incorporate your beliefs, your faith,
and what feeds you spiritually
into your home.*

If you are an atheist or an agnostic, don't skip this one. If you hate the word *God*, keep reading. This is about your beliefs, whatever they may be. Up to now, I've asked you to consider what makes you happy and your childhood. Now it's time to consider your beliefs as another critical pillar in the monument that is the home you will love. We're walking away from the stuff we have no connection to in favor of the meaningful. We're thinking about creating our space to honor all of who we are and what we do each day. Why on earth would we leave out our spiritual lives?

You will likely never see religious art in an interior design spread. Why is this? Perhaps designers and editors have decided that Judaic art is too personal, revealing too much about someone's beliefs. Or perhaps images of Jesus and the crucifixion are too disruptive to a coastal theme. (*Theme*, like *style*, is another word I don't care for in regard to a house. Birthday parties have themes; houses don't.) Whatever we find sacred belongs in our home and deserves prominence. The challenge is to find a way to express our faith in a manner that speaks to us aesthetically and spiritually, not to feel like we must hide it in a corner.

> In our home there was always prayer—aloud, proud, and unapologetic.
>
> —LYNDON B. JOHNSON

> God is at home, it's we who have gone out for a walk.
>
> —MEISTER ECKHART

> I believe in God, only I spell it Nature.
>
> —FRANK LLOYD WRIGHT

First you must ask yourself, *What is sacred to me?* We are growing as human beings on a journey every day. Sometimes the work on our spiritual lives is deliberate, sometimes it works us. Much of this work takes place inside our homes. Some of us regularly pray, meditate, and read spiritual texts—whether it is the Bible, *The Power of Now*, the Koran, or the *Big Book of Alcoholics Anonymous*. Whether we open our eyes and pray, reflect on the expanse of nature, or breathe through a Sun Salutation in the early morning, the artifacts of our belief system belong among us. Focus on what you believe and what you want to connect to, without judgment or worry that you're not doing it correctly or that you'll be questioned for your beliefs. This isn't about anyone else's needs or arguments. This is your house and your place of worship and spiritual connection.

Father Robert Barron, a noted contemporary author and speaker on the intersection of modern life and religion, says with respect to bringing faith into our daily lives, "Always begin with the beautiful. It leads you to the good, which leads you to the truth." I hear you, Father. We must find the beauty in our faith, live with it, and revel in it to connect and grow spiritually. If you can't find beautiful art and design connected to your beliefs, you've been looking in the wrong places. The act of finding a work of art, whether a tiny sculpture or a mural-size painting that speaks to you aesthetically and spiritually, is profoundly fulfilling. The finding is a journey in itself. It likely requires a search, perhaps a conversation with the faithful in your community, maybe even some travel. It requires you to know what brings you peace and what you find beautiful on a spiritual level. We've never had such easy access to such a diverse array of inspired art and expressions of faith. You are no longer limited to tiny religious stores or whatever your parents used to represent your spirituality. Be open to images of faith on your travels. Search websites like Etsy.com for handmade goods, have something made, or make something yourself. Don't be limited by what retailers may label as "religious" art. Consider nature, fine art, theater, music, sculpture, and literature as potential sources for objects, patterns, or images that speak to you on a spiritual level.

In addition to imagery, we can also express our beliefs through words. Thanks to printing technology, you can get anything you want printed as a wall decal, in any size, in any language, in any color, in any font. Find a poem or quote that moves you and inspires you, one that changes you after reading it, and put it on a wall in your home. I put the words of my favorite prayers on my walls in large type. I want to be reminded of these wise words as I walk by, and I want them to be some of the first words my children read. I usually bristle at something so trendy as the now ubiquitous vinyl decals. However, these decals can be created with words of your choosing—prayers or quotes or inspiring texts that fill your space with a different feeling than something unconnected to your beliefs. It's taking something available to you because of a trend and using it for something wholly unique. The best part may be that wall decals aren't permanent if you have a change of heart.

Surrounding yourself with images and objects that not only remind of you of your faith but encourage it elevates your house to one that helps you grow and develop as a human being. The inclusion of what is meaningful and faith-filled into your aesthetic is powerful for the feel of your home as well as the flow of daily life.

YOUR TURN
WHAT ABOUT FAITH?

1   *Where do you most want or need to be reminded of God or whatever spiritual source gives you strength? Are there spaces in your home that you see when you first arrive? Or that you look at while you are working? Or that you spend time in with family members? Where do you need to be fed the most?*

2   *What images or messages appeal to your spirit? Think about authors, poets, saints, and thinkers from all time periods. Consider images that are deemed divine by others and those that are not. What gives you strength? Could these images or messages be used more prominently in your home?*

3   *What do you want to do more of to work with your spirit? Do you need a space to pray? Practice yoga? Meditate? Be in nature? Read spiritual texts? Where can you make space for this?*

1

WHO WERE YOU?

Reconnect with your youthful spirit and
your passions of yesteryear.

If you fancy yourself very hip and still connected to the passions of youth—the music, culture, ideologies, and activities that enliven us before responsibility-laden adulthood yanks them away from us—skip this chapter. You're probably too cool for it. But if you're like me and have had mortgages or children or aging parents or professional demands that have rendered you utterly uncool and disconnected from the things you used to adore, let's look at those little lost loves—there are good ideas for your house there.

I've had four children in six years. Annual trips to Europe, learning about new music, most magazine reading, sleeping through the night on a regular basis, as well as connections to other hip adults began to recede from my life the day my first son was born. Even for the coolest among us, parenting often means leaving much of what we love behind. And it's not just parents who lose their cool. Age has a way of minimalizing much of what is so significant in youth, and that may be the worst part about it. We became the adults we are today by exploring those exotic places, obsessing over certain musicians, following artists or authors or comedians, keeping "busy" with hobbies that were dear to us.

Keeping the house hip requires you to regain contact with your cool. Even with a scene change to suburbia and less time to devote to youthful pleasures, you need to reconnect with a more youthful version of yourself. Many parents of young children migrate to bigger suburban homes, only to face white walls and empty spaces, not to mention a completely different set of organizational and functional needs, and no time to sit back and think, *How do I want this to feel and work and look?* Like all forms of self-expression, it becomes much harder to work on your house amid the responsibilities of adulthood. Add to that the fact that children wreck almost everything in their reach, and many people say, "The hell with it. What's eighteen years without a nice couch? I just won't look."

Get a nice couch. Get nice everything. And when I say nice, I don't mean expensive or extravagant or white (God help you). Nor do I mean right now. We're not buying anything for a while, remember? What I mean is, get the things you like, whether you have kids or not. If you have children, you will clock untold hours at home with them, even if you work outside the home. Better to be surrounded by things you love. Making your house work for you as an adult—the way you were, so to speak, in addition to the way you all are now—is important for your well-being. And children do better in spaces that are personal, reverential, and interesting. They do even better with happy parents.

A personal, soulful home takes time, and ideally draws equally from these three components: the glory days of the past, a possibly busy and bland present, and whatever the bright-eyed future holds. It will be painfully slow to put together—that's OK. The present shows itself without much work; it's the past that's hard. It's important to find those things that brought you pleasure before your children were born or something else kept you from them.

As slow as it may be to effect big change, small things can make a huge difference.

A good place to start is art. Art is often collected in a meaningful way: you are friends with the artist, someone gave you a painting you admired, you attended a gallery show you really liked, you

Age considers; youth ventures.

—RABINDRANATH
TAGORE

inherited the piece, or you just fell in love with something. Art is also associated with a specific time in our lives, perhaps a city or country where we used to live. Those reminders of your full life before becoming a parent and having too many bills to pay for art are important. Great rooms often start from just one meaningful piece. Art is also relatively unreachable. Even in a house with three boys, where nearly everything is a projectile, art usually goes unscathed. If you do nothing else, find the art you once loved, and find a place for it.

A client of mine, Hannah, was the daughter of a gallery owner and had compiled an impressive and diverse array of contemporary art. Most of it was in closets or stacked in corners on the floor, although a few hung on the walls here and there in her suburban split-level in New Jersey. She had hoped that a big move or a bigger renovation would be the time to use all that wonderful art, but neither came. The first thing I noticed in her home was one of the few paintings that was already on the wall, an oversized abstract canvas hung in the foyer. She mentioned that she loved the colors in it and that she always hung it up wherever she lived. Letting the art lead, I chose the boldest color in the piece—a deep, husky teal—and urged her to paint a prominent, windowless wall in her living room that color. This change invited other bold changes, including making her gorgeous baby grand piano the focal point of the room. Hannah found the formal adult space she was looking for through the art she already loved.

Another good prechild category to dive into is your time in college, graduate school, or some other educational situation when you put your whole self into learning without little people to interrupt you. This time in your life probably has books or other artifacts attached to it. If you are even moderately interested in the topics of your study, put those books out. I had a client who said to me, "Shouldn't my bookshelf be current?" "No," I replied, "it should be full of books you loved, love, and may love someday." Filling your home with your intellectual interests is powerful, even if you don't engage in or study or have much time for those topics today.

Another good place to go back to is your love life. This is most pleasant when you're still with the other parent of your children. If you are, find evidence and artifacts of your love before you both became parents or too busy. I found a series of photographs of my husband and me on prekid travels that I love to look at. I "arted" them up a bit Instagram-style and created a just-us gallery wall in our bedroom. This reminds us of a time when we were a couple alone. There is not one child's face in any of these photos. My kids love to look at them and comment on how skinny (and tan) both Mommy and Daddy look in all the photos.

If divorce or dry spells make your love life a sore subject you'd rather not use in your story, go to your interests, hobbies, or activities outside your career—especially those you used to really love that you have had to let go. So many people want to kayak, do yoga, paint, march in political rallies, or hike more often, but they can't because living with small children or caring for an elderly parent ensures there is no room for such triviality as a hobby. But these activities are important, even if they are on a hiatus. This is where your house can really bring back these things into your life.

Some of these activities require time away from home or money that isn't as disposable as it once was. Your house can't fix those issues entirely. But it can provide space, reminders, and inspiration. Is there something you used to do, that you'd like to do, inside your house? Where could you do it? It's helpful to start simple and think of one activity you'd like to do that has no connection with your present responsibilities. It doesn't matter if you sold your sewing machine or woodworking tools or whatever paraphernalia you need. Decide where in your house this hobby or fun activity or passion will be reborn as soon as it can be, and find a way to express it there and elsewhere in the house. I used to sew (tinker, really), and I've never really taken the time to learn techniques beyond simple stitches. Most anything to do with sewing, including large boxes full of notions, patterns, and fabric that I inherited from my grandmother, are in my attic, probably getting moldy. Someday I'll convert a large walk-in closet in my basement to a crafting and sewing space. For now, I use fabric swatches everywhere for everything: as coasters, on my bulletin board, in a box for my kids to play with. I collect fabric and old patterns. Someday I'll sew up a storm. For today, I gaze at my swatches and daydream.

YOUR TURN

BACK IN THE DAY

1 Name the five things you miss doing the most from a time
before children or big-time adult responsibilities.

2 Look at your answers to question 1 closely. If you miss sleeping
in, can you invest in your bedroom to make even child-filled
mornings feel luxurious? If you miss hiking in the mountains,
can you find a photo of your favorite place to hike and hang
it somewhere? If you said "dancing," can you give yourself a
dance floor inside your house? Can you invest in speakers?

3 Think about your top three experiences as a teenager or
twenty-something. Do you have artifacts from this time about
your house? You should!

8

WHAT'S YOUR MISSION?

*Get honest about what you want
from your life and home, and get
it on paper.*

Your home is more than just a building and furniture. It's the center of your life, even if you spend much of your daily life outside it. It's essential to be clear about what you're asking of your house well before you get to paint chips and fabric swatches and bids from contractors.

This is about elevating not just the furniture but your house as a whole to a sacred level. If all we wanted were our utilitarian needs covered (a working lavatory, a place to cook and store food, a mattress), this would be much simpler. We typically want much more than this. It's OK to want much more. What do you want the experience to be for those who live in or visit your home? What do you want your own experience to be? What do you want to have happen inside your home? What do you want to do there? This is far more complex than saying, "I want a traditionally styled living room."

Setting your intentions for your home now will make each decision going forward more meaningful and more connected to your best intentions for your life. Many of us are forlorn about not living our best life or not achieving what we want to achieve. We don't realize how much our house can have an impact here.

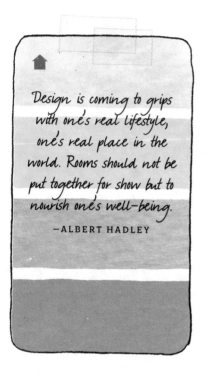

Design is coming to grips with one's real lifestyle, one's real place in the world. Rooms should not be put together for show but to nourish one's well-being.

—ALBERT HADLEY

Maybe you want to read more books or eat family dinners more often. Perhaps you're looking for a life partner or trying to have a family. Maybe you want to be more organized or enjoy the outdoors more. All of these goals can be helped and supported by designing your home well. Let your home work for you.

In our race to figure out what we want our homes to look like, we often forget to consider what we want our homes to do and how we want them to feel. Have you heard the phrase, "form follows function"? This is a concept from early modern architecture and design stating that the purpose or function of a space or object should drive how it looks, or its form. I prefer, "form follows function and is led by feeling." The early modernists hated any kind of decoration or aesthetic device unconnected to how something functions. They were delighted by anything utilitarian. I feel that decoration, or shapes, texture, and objects that shape the feeling, is in fact part of the room's function, and thus essential, so long as the feeling you are creating is desired and intentional.

Each space has a primary function and a secondary function. The more you consider what those are, the better equipped you'll be to make decisions that support those functions and make them more enjoyable. Perhaps the dining room is for special occasions, but also for high school algebra. The living room may be just as much for your sons to play *Halo* as it is for your book club. Think beyond the basics of shelter, hygiene, and nutrition. A lot of the functions are obvious, but consider what else you might like to do in your life. Do you want your house to inspire reading? Facilitate physical exercise? Calm you? Entertain you? Enable your obsession with baking? Allow you to have raucous parties? Before you think about anything visual, such as colors, textures, or furniture choices, write down what you want your house to do and what you ideally want to do in it.

Consider how you want your house to feel. You are creating a feeling, not just a composition (in design parlance)—or just a room for that matter. You're doing things that will cause your brain to stir and think and feel things. Rather than have that happen accidentally, think about the feelings you'd like to create. Do you want your house to feel calm and serene? Do you want it to feel buoyant and playful? How about both? Achieving the feeling you desire requires some good self-knowledge and awareness—and sometimes courage. Feelings are not universal. Your "calm" may be someone else's bland. Who cares. You need and deserve your own calm.

1   Find three to five adjectives or short phrases that describe how
you want your house to feel. Steer clear of tired adjectives like
warm, pretty, or inviting, *if you can.*

2   List each adjective in your Home Book and write out what each
means to you. For example, if you wrote, "I want my house to be
edgy," write what edgy means to you and take whatever time,
space, and words you need to express this.

3   If you can choose three of the most important functions of your
home (above and beyond the basics—shelter, safety, warmth),
what are they? These are about our ideal lives—connecting,
growing, developing, enjoying. What do you ideally want to say
happened in your home twenty years from now?

4   Based on your answers to questions 1-3, craft a mission
statement for your house—personal and unique, just like you.

If you're having a tough time with the preceding questions and coming up with a mission for your home, ask yourself these questions:

1   *If you are a parent, what are the three things you want most to teach your children?*

2   *What are you working toward in your personal or professional life?*

3   *Where do you see yourself and your family in the next five years? The next ten?*

4   *What kinds of activities or behaviors do you want your home to encourage every day?*

5   *What dreams and goals do you want your home to support?*

Write your home's mission as if it's already true, in the present tense, even if you feel it is far from that mission. Your house can't do everything, but your vision lays the groundwork for your home to do much more than it's doing today. Include what you want your house to do for you, what you need from it, and what you want from it. Words are powerful. Clarity about what you desire is half the battle in making your house what you want it to be. This mission statement is also a prayer, a wish, a desire for your home that asks what you need and want.

A treasure map is an actual, physical picture of your desired reality. It is valuable because it forms an especially clear, sharp image, which can then attract and focus energy into your goal.

—SHAKTI GAWAIN

9

THE HOUSE TREASURE MAP

*Visualize and create your fantasy
house with this useful tool.*

It's time to look inside yourself for the fantasy—not what someone else may call a "dream home" but what a dream home built entirely for you looks like. The treasure map exercise is about fleshing out the fantasy. Now that you've had time to think about your story, your rich heritage, and your travels, let's fantasize in that context. Imagine what a home that truly reflects you would be like. Not just something beautiful to look at, but a structure that would be an ode to you and your life. Think about the all-important questions: How do you want your house to feel? What does a space that would enable you to do all the things you want to do each day look like? Thanks to luxury design magazines, we have come to believe that luxury is a big house full of comforts and conveniences—indoor tennis courts, elevators, staff; a rote formula. True luxury is very personal.

For this exercise, you're going to make a collage. If you're wondering what this has to do with making your house better, stay with me. We're going to make a treasure map of your dream house. If you've read *The Artist's Way* by Julia Cameron, you are familiar with this powerful tool. There are other names for this exercise and other people have suggested it for all kinds of reasons, but essentially, the treasure map is a way to bring images that speak to you into a collage, into your consciousness, and then into your life. You can create a map for just one room or your entire house; it's up to you and where you are in your house-love journey.

Julia's version has you fantasize about the things you want for your life. In this version, you'll look for images that express what you want for your home. As you do this exercise, you will likely be reminded that you wanted to make a place for a dog someday or that you love the color teal. You may be drawn to pictures of windows or images of gardens. Whatever it is that grabs you, cut it out. I always end up cutting fabric from dresses or scarves. (Fashion magazines are very useful for this exercise because they are awash in textures and colorful drama.)

I can't promise you that the things you want will magically materialize. But I will tell you that this collage can really inform how you begin to make changes in your house. Sometimes imagery can stir ideas or remind us of what we haven't thought about yet. These images are personal, sometimes unexplainable. You are entitled to your own fantasies and dreams—you need not share them with anyone else unless you want to.

Don't overthink this exercise. It's meant to be fun, to add another set of images and ideas to the mix and allow you to be less than rational about your house for a moment. Before too long, it will be back to brass-tacks reality and lots of limitations, so take a moment to exercise a little creative fantasy. It's not *just* fun. This step, which may appear airy-fairy and whimsical, will also lead you to at least one good solution (if not more) for your real-life house.

1   *Get a stack of magazines. Look for qualities and attributes that really speak to you, and it need not be an image of a particular room or house. (You may find them in an advertisement for toothpaste.) Look for sensibility, not final result. Don't think about limitations—you have enough money, time, and the ability to live anywhere for this exercise.*

2   *Set the timer for twenty minutes and cut out objects, words, and people that appeal to you, imagery and concepts that express your fantasy house. You can be deliberate and actively look for pictures of gardens, or you can see what you're drawn to.*

3   *After the cutting time is up, create a collage. (I suggest making it on a large piece of paper, but if your Home Book is big enough, you can also create the collage right on its pages.) Don't make it perfect—this isn't an art project, and there is no grade.*

4   *Hang your collage or tuck it into your Home Book. Remember to date it. Don't be surprised if your collage looks and feels different than what you thought your house was supposed to look like.*

Part Two

YOUR HOUSE–FROM NUTS TO BOLTS

In Part One, you did a lot of critical thinking, the foundation of any solid design project. You considered who you are and what makes you happy, what home means to you and what you want from life inside your house. You also determined a mission for your house— what it must do for you. You now have the creative building blocks to take with you on every decision and every purchase for your home.

Whether you are a designer or a do-it-yourselfer, to love the house you're in, collecting information about you comes first. Getting clear on your home's assets and liabilities is a close second. This is the work of Part Two: research, data collection, and inventory taking that will help you see your home more clearly and position you to make big decisions later on. You will learn to balance respect for what your house has to offer with what you prefer, if those two things are in opposition. You'll look a little less inside yourself for a moment and a lot more closely at the space you're working with.

The intention of this section is twofold. First, I want to position you to see all that your house has to offer; to see it objectively; and to begin to understand, if not cultivate, real appreciation for the house as it is. Second, I want you to know your house better than anyone else does, so should you ever decide to hire a professional to do some bigger work, you can be the kind of client who gets the best out of whomever you hire.

We shape our buildings,
and afterwards our
buildings shape us.

—WINSTON CHURCHILL

10

WHAT'S THE STORY OF YOUR HOUSE?

*Research your home's history and
study it, not as a home owner, but as
a detective and an historian.*

If you're like most people, you have a hard time looking at your
house objectively. You may be well versed in its shortcomings
but have probably never taken an in-depth look at the house
itself. Many people have purchased their home because of its
neighborhood, school system, or affordability, and not for its
aesthetics alone. If you didn't buy your house for love and you're
not going anywhere anytime soon, it's time to take a look at the
object of your arranged marriage. It has a story and lovable
features too.

Unless you're an architectural historian, you may not know
the story of the building of your house, the architectural style
it represents, or much else about its life before you owned it. It
will take a little work, but it's worth finding out as much of this as
you can. It helps to see your home as architecture first. Once you
do, you'll see that there really is—or at least was—a purpose to
most things in your house, including those features you find ugly.
Opening your mind to what purpose or cultural norm yielded
your tiny kitchen or lack of closet space helps take the burden of
your house off you and puts it onto history. Do a little research on

your own home, broaden your understanding of architecture as a whole, and it will go a long way in helping you not only improve your home but see it with greater appreciation and understanding, which is a critical step toward house love.

Since the use of central air and cooling became a standard in new construction, for a couple of generations, we can now have any style home we want in any climate we want. These days, if you're custom-building a house, we ask, "Would you like a porch? A center-hall colonial? A fireplace in your bedroom?" This would sound absurd to our forebearers, whose homes were constructed entirely to balance the burden of the elements and extreme temperatures with building materials that were in short supply. What were once functional elements to heat and cool space are now aesthetic devices.

Your home probably doesn't predate mechanical heating and cooling, but the older your home is, the more its shape and contours were a function of a more restrained financial climate, less borrowing power for would-be home buyers, and building methods now considered inefficient and unnecessary. If your home is eighty or more years old, its architecture was likely driven by the availability of materials and climate control. You likely have plaster walls, older and outmoded electrical and heating/cooling systems, and much less closet space.

If your home is newer, its size and features are undoubtedly a function of a more powerful financial climate for borrowing and building bigger with greater efficiency. Since 1970, houses are built faster, with far less skilled labor and much greater profitability to homebuilders. Suburban flight, double-income families, more vehicles, and greater consumer borrowing power have lead us to bigger homes with walk-in-closets, master suites, and other grand bells and whistles from builders that have become the new construction standards.

Embrace your home's vintage, whether it's a postwar building-boom ranch or a 1980s cul-de-sac colonial, and come to learn the design story behind it. There are defined building styles—such as colonial, craftsman, Tudor, cape, and more—that your house may or may not fall into. Homes built after 1950 have less strict forms, and newer houses may borrow details from period styles here and there. If you notice a blend of styles or building techniques, identify which ones belong to the craftsman tradition, which are true colonial hallmarks, which belong to capes, and so on. As you start to identify the architectural style(s) in your home, you may decide you want to take a particular style further in your changes; in some cases, you may wish to water it down. It's helpful to be clear on what "it" is to do either of those things effectively. You may be inspired to research a particular design tradition further—craftsman homes born out of the Arts and Crafts movement of the early twentieth century are fascinating to learn about, for example. Learn as much as you can about your own home's tradition or about whatever style truly grabs you.

Consult your local municipality for any building or permit records that concern your address, and ask longtime neighbors about the history of your home. You can also learn a lot informally by looking within your house for clues to added-on spaces; layers of flooring or tile; and added or removed windows or doors, converted garages, and additions.

It is also helpful to learn the terminology of your home's many parts. Becoming conversant in basic home-building language radically changes your interactions with anyone you hire to work on your house. A home-building primer will help you whether you have DIY daydreams or not. For instance, understanding the difference between a load-bearing wall and a non-load-bearing wall with some accuracy greatly improves your ability to understand what's possible in your house. You may find that learning the basics of home-building bleeds into an interest in architecture and more attention lavished on buildings near you. I hope you can soon identify your favorite building in your town and call out its features by name. This connection with architecture will only make you a smarter and more open-minded home owner.

My other hope is that more learning will lead to acceptance, if not appreciation, of your home, even if you wish it were something else. Some elements can be altered to change the look and feel of the exterior of a home, others cannot—at least not without a considerable budget. A brand-new house can't always offer the perfect solution you're looking for, and in many cases, working with what you've got and understanding why it's there lead to more satisfaction. The more you learn, the more you'll understand what you can change, all the while developing appreciation for what is.

Study your house purely for its architectural and aesthetic merits. It may be the first time you've looked at it this way. Come to it as a visitor, and take it in brick by brick, so to speak. Commit to stripping away any biases or baggage you may have about your home. It is not too old or too new or too poorly constructed; it's not too ranch or too colonial or too small or too bland. It is your house, the object of your study, not ridicule—at least, not today.

Begin to really notice the elements of your home. Start outside. Stand in front of your home and consider these questions:

1   What does the outside of your home remind you of?

2   Is your front facade symmetrical? If so, can you amplify this feature somehow?

3   What's the first thing you notice? The second? The third? Do you like what you notice first?

4   Are all the windows the same shape? The same size?

5   What do you notice about the roof? What's it made of? Is there an overhang, where it extends beyond the structure of your house, or does it stop right with your house?

6   What kind of trim lines the windows and doors?

7   What is your house clad in? Vinyl siding? Wood siding? Brick? Stucco? Can you see details in the vinyl siding? Does the brick have any special characteristics (such as smooth, jagged, whitewashed)?

As you learn more about architecture, ask yourself these questions:

1 What's your favorite building (from anywhere in the world and any period in history)? Why?

2 What's your favorite house of all time (whether you've lived there or not, whether you've ventured inside or not)? Why?

3 What housing architecture styles are you particularly drawn to? Why?

Best Books on Architecture and Building

These are the best books I know of to learn about how new homes are made, what style home you have, and why homes are built the way they are.

A Field Guide to American Houses
by Virginia Savage McAlester and Lee McAlester (Knopf, 1984)

At Home: A Short History of Private Life
by Bill Bryson (Anchor, 2011)

The Homeowner's Glossary of Building Terms
published by the U.S. Department of Housing and Urban Development (http://publications.usa.gov /epublications/build-terms/terms.htm)

Housebuilding: A Do-It-Yourself Guide
by R. J. DeCristoforo (Sterling, 2007)

11

WHAT'S YOUR REAL ESTATE STORY?

Figure out your real estate position
and timing if it is unclear. (In other words,
get the resale monkey off your back.)

For some of you, this is the elephant in the room: How long will you be in your home? How likely are you to sell it and when? These are important questions to ask before you go any further. If you don't make a point of answering these questions, you'll carry around the real estate monkey wherever you go, throughout this book and in whatever you do in your house.

Your own personal timing is the most important factor to consider in whether changes to your home are a good investment. More than your local market's idiosyncrasies or what real estate media tells you about shifting home values, if you don't get clear on your timing, resale value anxiety will never leave you. *Resale*, used casually as in, "I can't, I have to think about resale," is shorthand for "the gnawing anxiety that something may hurt me if and when I go to sell even though I don't know when that is but am forced to be ready for at all times." Resale will question every change you make. It will make you wonder if what you want will harm your home's value before you discern how much you need it or will enjoy it. It's important to reframe the question. How long you're likely to use and enjoy a new bathroom or an addition is just as important a consideration as how it will affect the resale.

If you stay plugged in to real estate media and fail to discern and decide about your own timing, you'll probably become too afraid to do anything. The fear of negative real estate implications is the most common reason for home paralysis. The desire to please an unknown buyer who may appear three, five, even ten years from now—and in doing so realize untold appreciation in a home's value—drives many people to either do nothing or follow a real estate professional's playbook with what to do with their homes, as if any real estate professional could know what a visitor ten years from now will want. Why should we do what *we* want? We should do what *those people* want. The people who'll likely buy our house. Whoever they are. Whenever that is.

Real estate professionals are lovely people who make their living selling homes. They are not the people to ask whether you should move or not, whether you'll be happy in your current house forever, or whether you'll regret a big addition you're considering. They cannot tell you what's best for your family or even what's possible in the house they're showing you, with certainty. They may very well say that this or that house is really best for your kids, that you should jump on an opportunity because it would be great for your family, or better yet, you could easily add on here. (Add-ons are rarely easy.)

I don't blame real estate professionals for acting as life gurus when it comes to guiding someone in or out of real estate. Their job is to make us feel comfortable and at ease with what society has turned into a very stressful process. Our national consciousness is fraught with anxiety and fear when it comes to our homes, and this has become much worse since 2008. What has always mattered, and what matters most today, are your personal needs and quirks when it comes to buying your home. Remember that your house is a home first and an asset second.

Take the information you have today and determine, without outside factors, how long you can stay in your current home. Assuming no job transfers, no lottery wins, no surprise triplets, and no military deployments, how long will your current house work for you? I know there are problems, but set them aside for a moment. There are really only two categories: we'll leave in the next five years, and we'll stay at least five years.

Once you know how long you'll be in your home, consider how fast you want to make changes. Here is one way of thinking about it: if you are only going to be there a short time, get cracking. Start prioritizing and project planning to ensure you are the primary beneficiary of any updates or changes. From a financial position, you'll be able to amortize the value of any improvements you do and thus make the most of the home you're in today. You'll also make the most of your house for your life as it is for the next five or so years; you can tailor a house to suit that span of time.

If you plan to be there forever, you can wait. Forever houses go much more slowly, and that's how it should be. It's easy to visualize life over the next five or eight years. Even if you have a baby or two in that span of time, you can still see what your needs may be. With any

> Be sure you put your feet in the right place, then stand firm.
> —ABRAHAM LINCOLN

> Fear keeps us focused on the past or worried about the future.
> —THICH NHAT HANH

longer time spans, all bets are off. It's tough to fully understand what life will be like. It takes thinking and discernment—the long view.

If you are in your "this is it" house, I hope you endeavor to personalize every square inch and take your time to make the whole that is the house entirely yours. But this takes time, thought, intention, and money. My neighbor from Summit, New Jersey, Mrs. Dabella, is a lovely woman who bought a tiny cape and transformed it into an enormous stone-clad home exactly to her liking, including hand-painted likenesses of her children on the kitchen tile. She said, "They are carrying me out of this house in a box. I will work on making it mine until then." This perspective offers so much, but it also provides a tremendous challenge. A forever house? What does that even look like for you? Take your time, if that is where you find yourself; it takes a long time to know the answer.

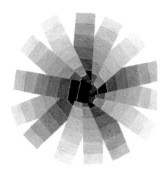

Consider the following statements and write the one that best
describes you in your Home Book. Note that most of the reasons listed
don't have much to do with the house itself. Houses can be fixed up,
added to, or improved. Commutes and schools usually can't, at least
not quickly enough. Nowhere do I ask you to consider the local real
estate market. Look inward, speak with your partner, find out which
list represents your situation, regardless of what's going on in your
neighborhood. This is an important, weighty decision, not one that
anyone else can make for you. And once you choose one side of the
five-year horizon, it will make the rest of your work here much easier.

We're staying at least five years.

- We like the school system or access to private
  schools.
- Our commute is acceptable or better.
- The access to amenities is acceptable or better.
- We like our neighbors.
- The people who matter to us are close.
- We're comfortable here, even though we don't think
  we can stay forever.
- We need time to save for a down payment before we
  buy another house.

- We don't know precisely what we want or where we want to go.
- There are things about the house that work, even though there are many things that don't.

We're leaving in the next five years.

- The local school system doesn't work.
- Our commute has to change.
- We don't have enough bedrooms for the number of people in our family.
- Our house is too expensive.
- We've saved enough to buy a larger house without having to sell our own first.
- The majority of the house in terms of layout, space, and function doesn't work for our needs.

Can you commit to your house for five years or more? This may sound scary, as commitment is coupled with investment in a house you surely aren't in love with or you wouldn't be reading this book. Commitment is liberating and engaging, however. It allows you to land somewhere and to focus on where you are. It also yields great, confident, focused results in design and problem solving around the home.

12

GET YOUR HOUSE ON PAPER–
AND IN PICTURES

*Arm yourself as the pros do—create
accurate floor plans and a full set of
photographs so you have your home's
details at your fingertips at all times.*

If you are detail-oriented and like to draw, you're going to like this
one. If you like numbers, you're going to love it. It's time to get
your house down on paper. Architects and designers must have
an accurate floor plan, drawn to scale, to work on your house.
Even if you don't want to make substantial changes to the walls
or the structure of your home, this is an essential tool for making
decisions about furniture purchases, furniture arrangement, and
the flow of rooms that have multiple entryways. Designers always
take a lot of photographs too, so they can recheck details or
intricacies of your home without having to visit again. Taking lots
of pictures of your home will do something else; it will let you be
creative in a different way than when you're standing in the space.
For maximum benefit, do both—draw your own floor plan, and
photograph every square inch of your home.

A floor plan will provide a bird's-eye view of your home, or
at least one floor of it. I suggest having a drawing that shows the
entire first floor or whatever floor gives you the most trouble, as

well as separate drawings for any rooms you are working on. This involves a lot of sketching, measuring, and note taking, as well as some math. If you're up for it, you will be able to use the result for doing any kind of purchases, solving furniture placement conundrums, or figuring out how to make tough rooms work.

Take your floor plan with you when you go shopping. You'll know whether a couch you like will fit and in how many different positions you can place it just by having all of the room's measurements and knowing where the windows and doors are located. You'll be able to buy or order curtains, because you'll know the width of the windows and how many there are, as well as the ceiling height if you are planning on hanging the curtains higher than the windows. You will also know how big each room is in square feet, which is useful when buying flooring or paint. If you stop here, well done! You'll use this tool forever, especially if it's neat and tidy. Make a zillion copies of it.

If you want to go further and create a draft to scale, this is a different kind of tool with even more applications for making your house great. With a to-scale drawing, you can manipulate it for future possibilities. Print or photocopy your floor plan, and either sketch out ideas on vellum placed over your drawing or write directly on it. If you enlarge your copy, make sure to keep the scale recorded on the drawing.

I like to feel things out on paper. I have floor plans for every room in my house, and for some rooms, I have multiple possible layouts with different options sketched on paper. I love these drawings, especially once a room is finished and I can see it from drawing to completion. For instance, my sons share a small room. I created a to-scale floor plan of this room and had to play a Tetris-like game to figure out a way to fit in three beds, including a set of bunk beds. I ended up with all sorts of configurations, and because I had the dimensions of the furniture we owned and planned to keep, plus accurate measurements of the room, I could play around with different options to see what would work best. In my mind, a particular layout seemed interesting and striking. On paper, I saw right away that it was too crowded, with too small a space between the beds. I need everything laid out on paper because my mind's eye does not always get scale right.

I prefer drawing to talking. Drawing is faster and leaves less room for lies.

—LE CORBUSIER

If this sounds like a lot of work for you, it is. But it's worth it. There is nothing worse than getting a new piece of furniture delivered only to find that it doesn't fit where you thought it would. If you have all your measurements on hand, even if your drawing is not to scale, this will never happen. If you have a full set of photographs, you can also avoid a lot of pitfalls: you'll be reminded of where your outlets are, roughly how much space is between the windows, or how tall the fireplace is. There are a lot of steps for creating a proper floor plan for our purposes, but it has a long shelf life and will come in handy no matter what you do with your house.

Grab a pencil and some paper (graph paper is ideal), invest in a good-quality tape measure, and invite a friend over for pizza. Digital distance measuring tools are useful for long distances, and if you have one, you can do this alone. However, partners are helpful for recording all the measurements and keeping you company.

1   First, sketch the shape of the entire first floor and how it's divided into separate spaces. Don't worry about being exact—only the shapes are important in this step; the scale is not. Try to draw the longer walls longer than the shorter walls, and place the doors and windows generally where they exist in reality. This is just your first draft, onto which you'll jot all the measurements. Make sure you don't miss any angles or bump-outs or things that make a space less than a perfect square or rectangle. Use the symbols on page 67 to help make your drawing a bit clearer.

2   Once you have your outlines, of either a specific room or an entire floor, with the interior walls, windows, and doors sketched in, start measuring. First measure the width of each wall—essentially the length and width of the room. If possible, I like to measure length and width while putting the tape

measure on the floor as opposed to taking the measurements from halfway up the wall. This way, I am including the added girth of the baseboard trim, which typically protrudes about one inch. (In small spaces, one inch per side matters!)

3   Measure the widths of windows and door openings. I like to measure windows and doors using the widest measurement, meaning outside the window or door trim, the molding that surrounds most windows and doors. A professional survey would measure the trim separately and express the trim, as well as the windows and doors, to scale in the final, as-built drawing. That's not necessary for this exercise, but it is important to include trim in your measurements.

4   Measure how high the windows are above the floor. You can write "AFF" (above finished floor) to be official and indicate this vertical measurement in your floor plan. This measurement will tell you what could fit underneath the windows and also how long curtains should be, if you're buying those.

5   Measure the ceiling height of the room. If it changes, note where the ceiling dips or is higher in one area.

6   If you have built-in lighting fixtures on the wall or in the ceiling, note where these are and measure accordingly.

7   Don't forget your closets! If you plan to organize them in the future with shelving, a system such as Elfa from the Container Store, or even a custom solution like California Closets, it helps

to know their overall plan view (or bird's-eye/overhead view) measurements. The elevation view (or view looking straight ahead at eye level) will be just as valuable, however, in planning for shelving or hanging bars and so on.

8 *Move on to the next room, if applicable.*

9 *Assuming your first draft is messy and hard to read, make a second draft that is neater and larger, or try drawing the whole thing to scale with graph paper.*

PHOTOGRAPH YOUR SPACE

Taking pictures is easier and just as valuable if not more so. The rule here is that you can't have too many. Take a set of photographs of each room that includes every wall in that particular room, and stand approximately ten feet away from the wall. (The goal is to include the whole wall in the photo.) In addition to the four (or so) wall photos per room, photograph well-lit detail shots of the flooring or any other materials in the space—such as brick, stone, or tile—as well as any built-ins or other features, even if you hate them. Last, take a wide view, if possible, of the room from the vantage point of the entrance, including as much of the room as possible. You can keep these photos on your smartphone, which makes things easy when you're shopping. You can also print them all out and keep them in your Home Book. They provide extraordinary clarity if printed out. Take photos of your exterior as well; they are essential for landscaping or making any changes outside. Your thoughts about what works or what needs changing will undoubtedly change after seeing your home in photos.

Floor Plan Symbols

Floor plans are composed of symbols. You can learn the symbols the pros use, or you can make up your own (just remember to note what each one means). If you are drawing the entire first floor, use thicker lines to express the exterior perimeter walls of your house and thinner lines to express the interior walls that carve up the space inside. Here are other helpful symbols:

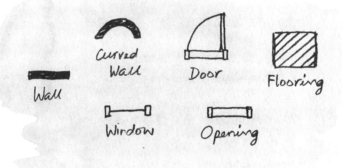

Wall

Curved Wall

Door

Flooring

Window

Opening

Have nothing in your homes that you do not know to be useful and believe to be beautiful.

—WILLIAM MORRIS

13

TAKE STOCK OF YOUR STUFF

Categorize the contents of your home.
Decide what you love and what has to go.

Every successful retail business has intimate knowledge of its inventory: what's selling, what's sitting, and where everything is stored. Do the same thing when it comes to your home. Take an inventory, not just of the contents of your house but also of your relationship to each of the things you own. Ideally, we would only own things that have great meaning to us, things we love. This is a wonderful goal, but it takes time and doesn't happen overnight. You can't always go out and replace everything you have but don't love, and you shouldn't anyway. Loving everything you own means that each item is meaningful and loved over time, not in one shopping spree.

Some of us are too attached to *placeholder buying*. It goes something like this. You think, *I can't afford a nice couch, but we need a place to sit, so let's buy this cheap one just to have something.* Or it may be, *I hate this dining set from my mother-in-law, but I don't have anything else to put in the dining room.* Or, *This armoire is broken, but I'm waiting until I can buy something nicer.* Sometimes this attitude of "I just can't get a better table/chair/desk/lamp right now" bleeds into everything in your house and takes over. You end up holding on to items out of habit; you might even forget why you still own them or that they're supposed to be temporary. Most of us think we need more furniture than we actually do. The key is to get clear on each piece and its purpose, then make a plan to clear out the stuff that doesn't work for you. Even if you have something in your home you don't particularly love but don't care to part with, get clear on your relationship to that piece, how you feel and what your plan is to replace it in the future.

I like my things in three categories: I Love It, Placeholder, or Pass It On. (Notice there is no category for "I own it because someone gave it to me, and I can't throw it out because they'll be upset." This category is also called Pass It On.) These three categories acknowledge that I can't replace or get rid of everything that isn't perfect (to me) in my house, but it maintains the ideal that someday I will. I don't think it's so unreasonable to imagine a house where you love everything—not just when you win the lottery, but over time, as you know yourself and collect things for your home. This isn't so much the state of being done but the state of knowing what you love and need so well that you're able to put the vast majority of things into the I Love It category.

What will be the most useful is the list of items in the I Love It column. The goal is not to focus on what you feel you must replace; it is to get clear on what you love. Do you have a lot of things you are just ho hum about? Do you think it's unnecessary to love the things that surround you every day? Are you ambivalent or dispassionate because someone else picked out items for you? There is a trap that occurs when someone else picks out things for you. Not always but often someone else's passion for an object— whether it's a designer, your mother, or a friend—rather than your own true feelings leads you to a purchase. But it's not for their house—it's you that has to live with it all. This exercise is meant to help you identify what you truly love and care about, not what someone else thought was interesting at some point in the past.

There are those of us who like to hold on to things "just in case." In case you can't buy another one, or your grown child needs them when he gets his own apartment, or you add on to your home, or your grandmother comes back from the dead and asks you what you did with her sewing table. If this is where you are, that's OK. I'm not going to make you get rid of something that doesn't have value to you, but these items belong on the Pass It On list. In your mind and on your list, acknowledge that they are not for you, even if you can't take the action to get rid of them. Understand though, that holding on to things you don't like has a financial and psychological cost. Someone else may be looking for just the thing you're holding on to. Make space for better stuff just for you.

This exercise is great for people who've inherited a lot of their furniture. A lot of times we keep things because we think we should, we were told to, or we are afraid of trusting our gut. Keep what you like, and donate the rest. There are furniture thrift stores that pick up from your home, and other organizations like Habitat for Humanity's ReStores and the Vietnam Veterans of America will gladly take used furniture off your hands, so long as it isn't broken, in exchange for a tax receipt. Often the latter makes more economic sense, especially if it's not your cup of tea to meet strangers at your house and haggle with them the Craigslist way.

Take out your House Book and put "I Love It" at the top of one page. Write "Placeholders" on top of another page, and put "Pass It On" on a third page. Start with the room that gives you the most trouble— most likely it contains things you don't care for. Inventory everything in the room, starting with the biggest pieces. There is a reason why the categories are not nuanced. Do you love it or not? If you don't love it but you have no intention of giving it away, it's a placeholder. You don't need to know how you'll replace it. You don't need to know exactly how or when you'll purchase a new sofa/armoire/coffee table/ chair. But categorizing opens your eyes to what you are working toward in your house. It also helps you understand why you have certain things.

When you have your list of loved things, consider why you love each one. Is it the inherent shape and contour of the piece? Is it because it was given to you by a loved one? Is it because you got a great deal on it? Is it because it looks sophisticated? Is it because it reminds you of a specific time in your life? Is it because it just works like it was made for its location? Does it make you smile? Once you know what you love, you can build on that with future decisions.

CREATE A CLEAR VIEW

If you prefer to work with your hands and you're a very literal person, this exercise is for you. This will give you an opportunity to look closely at your stuff, and it will help you create a new vision for a room you may be stuck with. Consider moving everything out of a room you're struggling with. Seeing a space empty is an invitation to erase any ideas you have about it, see the assets of that space laid bare, and be open to what else can be done with it. Take in the room after the removal of each piece of furniture and decoration. Sometimes just the removal of a single large, cumbersome, unloved piece of furniture will help you see your space differently, but the more you move out the better. As you work, answer these questions:

1   *Once empty, what is the first thing you notice about this space?*

2   *Where does the natural light come from? And when?*

3   *What are the natural passageways in and out now that furniture is no longer there?*

4   *Do you like the room empty? Sometimes there is a nice quality to an empty room that may inspire you to put back less when you eventually bring in your furniture.*

5   *Would you consider using the space in a different way or for a different purpose?*

Live in or among the empty spaces for a few days. Even if you simply return what was already there, you'll do it more thoughtfully, with clearer intentions, and most likely, with less stuff.

14

WHAT DO YOU LOVE ABOUT YOUR HOUSE?

*Pivot your attitude about your house
to the positive, and catalog the things
you love about your home.*

What does your home offer? Perspective goes a long way here.
If you are hyperfocused on what's wrong or broken or too small,
you miss opportunities to play up your home's best qualities.
Furthermore, you can get lost in negativity about your house. Stop
calling it a dump or a disaster or ugly. It may not work for you right
now, but you can make it work better. This likely won't happen by
bulldozing it and starting over. It will come from figuring out what
you do appreciate and building on that, cultivating gratitude about
the house you have. Gratitude will propel the creative process in
finding solutions and expressing yourself more fully in your home.
If you're stuck in negativity, the ideas just don't come.

Do you like the way light enters a particular room? The way
big trees shade your backyard? Your azaleas in the springtime?
Do you have the perfect spot for a Christmas tree? Do you have
a great fireplace? A generous closet? These bright spots around
your home can involve the raw space itself or how furniture you
love works in a space. You can love the way things work together—
beloved furniture pieces in a corner of the house that was made
for them, for instance. Often it's parts of the house that work with

> Gratitude unlocks the fullness of life. It turns what we have into enough, and more. It turns denial into acceptance, chaos to order, confusion to clarity. It can turn a meal into a feast, a house into a home, a stranger into a friend.
> —MELODY BEATTIE

things we love that makes spaces we really enjoy inside our home.

Ask the other people you live with what they like. My sons love the attic-bedroom that my daughter currently inhabits. They think it's cool that the roof slopes down to the floor and that there are lots of nooks and crannies in the room for hiding. I think this room is more appropriate for hobbits than for humans, but they think it's great. And their opinion helps me to see it differently. My husband loves our tiny living room with its gas fireplace, which he installed. He loves to lie down in the TV-free room, fire ablaze, and relax. Were the room any bigger, more people—especially little people and their toys—would find him. But because it's small and mostly an adult space, he usually inhabits it alone and peacefully.

Carefully shed the negative opinions others have about your house. Sometimes we have a distaste for our house because of what others have said to us. Or perhaps our discomfort with what we have comes from what others have said about split-level homes, older homes, or yellow homes—whatever it is we have that others have labeled unfashionable or wrong in some way. This is a time to tune in to what you like, what you appreciate, and what you find beautiful, letting go of what others think and specifically of how they perceive beauty. (They don't live there or pay the bills!)

Focusing on what you enjoy looking at and what you find interesting, endearing, or comfortable in your home, make a list. Find ten things you love about your house. They can be small details, spaces, rooms, particular windows, corners, seasonal effects, and so on. It's up to you. Put them in your Home Book in a list titled "Ten Things I Love about Our Home Today" and date it. It's useful to ask your partner and children, if they are old enough to read and write, to do the same exercise; they may appreciate very different aspects of your home. The gratitude of others is like fertilizer for your gratitude, especially in the home.

Once you have your list, you may want to rip it out of your Home Book and tape it up somewhere. There may be small projects or things you can do to augment or play up the aspects that you like so much. Whether you make them even better or leave them alone, your list of ten things you love in your home today will be instrumental in guiding you to make changes elsewhere.

15

WHAT DO YOU HATE ABOUT YOUR HOUSE?

*Time to vent! List all your grievances in
a way that directs you toward action,
resolution, and improvement.*

My four-year-old loves the word *hate*. There must be something
about saying, "I hate this/you/him/carrots" that gives him
comfort. As much as I dislike being on the receiving end of this,
I understand the easy release in saying you hate something. It's a
way to communicate words and feeling, all in a neat little package.

If you really hate your house or have trouble with most of it,
it was probably a challenge to come up with a list of ten things
you love. But it's key to change not only our homes but our
perspectives as well, and calling out the good first helps to shift to
the positive. Now it's time to vent but in a useful way.

Zero in on what you don't like with all the vim and vigor of an
angry four-year-old, but go further. Tune in to the why. Does your
hatred come from comparing your house to the homes of others?
Don't compare and despair. When you vent and make your list of
things you hate, make sure the things you hate are things that really
don't work for you, not things that just don't seem to measure up.

I worked with a great family, the Lances, who lived in a good-
sized house with lots of problems. Their kitchen, a disaster, was
causing marital strife. They illustrated for me what it was like for the

From the deepest desires often come the deadliest hate.

—SOCRATES

husband and wife to cook together. It was a little like watching two grown people inside a pinball game, with both spouses trying to get out of each other's way and bumping into things in the process. "So many fights are caused by this stupid kitchen," Ken Lance told me. "It's got to go first, even though we have so many things we could do at the same time." I agreed. Although they hated their front entrance, their bedroom, and their living room, they hated their kitchen and what it was doing to their relationship the most.

It's more than fair to survey your partner, or whoever else pays the mortgage or rent, for his or her hates. Spouses often hate different things for different reasons. It's important to get it all out. It's also important to find any of the things you both hate or both struggle with first. These are ideal projects to tackle before getting into more personal pet peeves about the house.

When you're making your hate list, consider usage and frequency as well. Most of us use our kitchens multiple times every day. The guest bedroom might be heinous beyond redemption, but if you don't have occasion to use it very often, it shouldn't be at the top of your list. When we moved into our house, we somewhat foolishly redid the basement first. Yes, it needed to be done, but it got done because I wanted my mother to be more comfortable (and less disgusted) every time she came to visit and had to sleep down there. Rather than offer her an upstairs space in which to sleep and focus on another problem that may have been more meaningful, I addressed the shame and discomfort of disappointing my mother—or rather the chance to try and make her a happier houseguest. Don't fall into this trap. This is the Thanksgiving trap, working on your dining room so that four hours on one day in one year can be more pleasant for guests. Focus on things that affect you the most, emotionally if need be, on most of the days of your all-important existence. Others will get over any shortcomings they experience during a visit much more easily than you will.

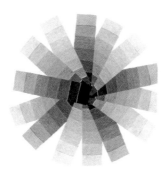

Pull out your Home Book and make a list titled "Ten Things I Hate about Our Home Today." Make this an enjoyable, thoughtful exercise. Think about why you hate something in your house, even if the reason is "This room is just ugly," but try to go deeper than that. Be clear about precisely what you dislike.

As you create your list, try putting the things you hate in a particular order. Your list needs to reflect how much you hate something based on how much you feel that sense of discontent or frustration and how often. The things at the top of your hate list should be the things that cause you the most negative feelings day in and day out. These are things that you are in contact with every day or multiple times a day. Not just eyesores but things that are functionally broken.

Next, go over the list with your spouse/partner. For each item ask yourselves, if you could change one thing about the object of hatred, what would it be?

16

WHERE DO WE BEGIN?

Systematically prioritize the projects or problems you want to tackle in your home.

By now I hope you've gained a bit of "housetrospection." This comes from a deep look inside your home to see what's lovable, what's redeemable, and what absolutely must change. For most of us, prioritization is very hard. Often people reach out to me by e-mail, saying they need design help in a few spaces in their home. When I press them to send me a prioritized list, they may send me two or three different lists with rearranged priorities. It's hard to pick what to do first: some days doing the bathroom first is a no-brainer; other days you think you'll die if you don't repaint the outside. Still, there is an order that works for every family. Having your list, just like getting clear on your real estate status or anything else you commit to, will make it easier to move forward. No more "I don't know what to do first."

I am no stranger to wanting all my problems fixed yesterday and to the difficult job of prioritizing. Our relationship with our home is not purely rational. There are emotional factors that make it tough to prioritize well. Prioritizing is an exercise in being reasonable while allowing your heart a vote or two. Tease out the reasonable list of projects based on what you know of yourself, your needs and desires, and what your house has to offer as assets and challenges, then make sure it all feels right for you and anyone who lives with you.

There is no universal list that works for everyone. Like everything else to do with your home, this activity is very personal. Take on the projects that will net you the greatest positive impact on your *daily* life first. I consider feeling good when you drive up to your home each day a very positive impact. (Don't leave your heart out of this.) So this is not all about fixing what's functionally broken, unless fixing what's functionally broken will have the greatest impact.

Let's pretend this is our yet-to-be-prioritized list of home projects:

- *Make the basement usable—paint, put flooring down, add lighting*
- *Update the girls' room—swap out baby furniture for bed, dresser, and so on; paint*
- *Refresh front exterior entrance with lighting fixtures, paint, and so forth*
- *Make dining room usable—buy table, chairs, hutch; paint; put up new lighting fixture*

Consider the rational, emotional, and financial reasons for tackling each of these projects. The quiz at the end of this chapter will walk you through this. The answers are personal, and I can't tell you which project belongs first, second, third, and so on. There is no magic order or wrong answer. If this were your house, perhaps the basement would score well functionally, the dining room emotionally, and the entrance project from a real estate standpoint. You have to decide what drives you in terms of the change you want to see in your home. The cost and mechanics of any project also impact where they belong on the priority list.

Each project should be viewed with a cost estimate attached when you are prioritizing. You can do some research online or make preliminary calls to contractors, but have a ballpark figure, such as painting your front door and installing new light fixtures will likely cost about $500. Also consider the mechanics of getting the project done. How long will the space be out of commission? Can the project be done in any weather? How disruptive to daily life will the project be? With large-scale construction projects and complex renovations, your life is upended. With smaller projects, even just a paint job in the dining room, daily life doesn't exactly stop, but it is disrupted. When you're considering each project, think about what it will entail. For instance, for the girls' bedroom redo listed earlier, you might include ordering and receiving furniture, moving the girls out for about a week, and coordinating painters and electricians. Perhaps this is a project best suited for the summertime, when our hypothetical girls are out of school. When you prioritize, consider everything associated with a project. It's frustrating to get geared up and ready to do something only to realize that you have to wait for different weather or more ideal family timing.

Feel free to change your mind as you go. You may have your list but find it hard to hire the best contractor. Go to your number-two project if you wish. Your Home Book is the perfect place to keep your very dynamic, very fluid priorities list. A change of seasons may help you see your priorities differently. In spring, the outdoor projects seem timely; in the fall, everything inside beckons. If you have thought it through and checked in with your heart, have your list, and are ready to move forward, well done! Remember, this is your house, so make it yours. Unless the answers are really clear, don't do more than one big project a year unless you have to, especially if you're in your forever house. Forever houses take lots and lots of time, careful thought, and lollygagging to become great for the long haul.

YOUR TURN
THE PRIORITIES QUIZ

This exercise takes writing and conversation with your partner. Create a list of the home projects you'd like to tackle, then work through the following questions.

The first things to consider are the functional reasons for the project. If the problem you want to tackle does one of these things, assign it five points:

1 *The problem creates a safety issue for my family (such as broken steps, flooring, windows, or doors).*

2 *The problem is costing additional money in utility, plumbing, electrical, or handyman bills (leaky bathrooms, old or broken windows, and so on).*

3   *The problem causes unacceptable discomfort in the home related to temperature (for example, old or broken windows, poorly sealed doors, faulty HVAC system, poor insulation).*

4   *The problem presents risks to the integrity of our home and could cause long-term damage or costly problems in the future (roof problems, foundation problems, and so forth).*

5   *The problem doesn't allow us to use our house or property to its full potential (such as no access to the yard, an unfinished basement).*

Next, consider the emotional reasons for each project. If the problem does one of these things, assign it four points:

1   *The problem is unattractive, and we spend a lot of time looking at it (broken or poorly maintained outdoor or indoor elements, things that scream an era you're not fond of, and so on).*

2   *The problem will make it difficult, once again, to have my annual Christmas party comfortably in three months.*

3   *The problem makes me embarrassed when people come over.*

4   *The problem makes our house stand out as less attractive in our neighborhood, and that bothers me.*

5   *The problem makes me ashamed of my house.*

6 The problem reminds me of a former owner/spouse/loss.

7 The problem is something my mother/mother-in-law/neighbor/
best friend pointed out.

8 The problem creates or adds to family chaos or friction
between family members.

Finally, consider the real estate and financial reasons of each project.
It won't surprise you that these get the fewest points. They are
valid, but they are not change drivers as much as they are change
supporters. If your problem does any of these things, assign it two
points:

1 My real estate agent told me that if I took care of this problem,
my house would go up in value.

2 A house just like mine sold easily because it had taken care of
this problem.

3 Everyone who has the same house in my development took
care of this problem, and I like the results.

4 Solving this problem will make our house more marketable
someday when we sell.

5 We can easily finance the solution to this problem.

Reorder your list from most points to least—this is your new priority list. If you like, make a nice, neat little chart and determine what scores best, what you can afford easily, ideal timing, and so on.

VISUALIZING CHANGE

What if the preceding exercise doesn't result in the list you want? Sometimes I need a little more nuance and a little more freedom to work on feeling. Close your eyes, and visualize each project done as well as you can imagine at this moment, even if it's a fantasy-like change.

- *How many times a day do you enjoy your new change?*
- *How great does it feel to look at it?*
- *How does your day function differently with this change in place?*

These emotions are impossible to quantify but useful, as your feelings after this visualization may shift your priorities list a bit. The heart does not lie, as we are fond of saying in our house. Certain things can line up to make perfect sense, but it just isn't what we want to do first. That's OK.

The Case for Little Wins

Although I will never tell you which project to do first, I will make a strong case for the little wins. Often when you feel overwhelmed by all the large projects you know you must take on in your home, little wins make a huge difference and mellow out the anxiety you may feel for the large projects. Allow yourself to have the little-big wins. Are there small things you can do to bring a smile to your face every day? Is there a Venn diagram with two circles that intersect—one containing projects that don't cost a lot of time or money, and the other with projects that would make you happy—for your house? When these two circles of options intersect, what's in the middle? What projects are quick, inexpensive, and a big boost for your house comfort?

> Start by doing what's necessary; then do what's possible; and suddenly you are doing the impossible.
> —FRANCIS OF ASSISI

17

TO ADD OR NOT TO ADD?

*Learn addition basics and whether they
are a viable option for you, your lifestyle,
and your pocketbook.*

Maybe you've had the add-versus-move conversation. You need
more space, but you don't want to move. Or you want to move,
but you can't afford a bigger, better house. Sometimes moving is
less expensive than adding on—of course, it depends on where
you move to and how big your addition is. Sometimes adding on is
simpler and cheaper than moving. Deciding whether to add or not
is a delicate and complex thought process, a bit of a black box for
most home owners that I want to demystify. Here are eight things
to keep in mind if you are considering an addition.

1. *The government has a (big) say.* Find out the rules that pertain
to your property as soon as possible. Additions are subject to a
municipal permitting process as well as zoning restrictions. If your
home is older, the addition may be subject to different regulations
of space, electrical requirements, or other rules that the original
home was not. You might not be able to add on at all due to your
lot size, where your neighbors are, or how far your setbacks are.
(Setbacks are the boundaries delineating just how far out to the
side or in front you can build.)

2. *It's always more expensive than you think.* Adding the raw space is not expensive. The materials alone (lumber, insulation, hardware, and so on) are not costly. Even the labor on its own is not what makes an addition expensive. It's the combined costs of permits, design fees, building, and integrating the addition into your existing structure that make additions pricey. It's not that you're adding that twelve-by-fourteen bedroom; it's that your entire roof needs to be removed to do so.

3. *It's true that it's less expensive to build on top of something that's already there, but you can't always do it.* You will probably need an expert to tell you whether you can build on top of existing one-story space. A closed porch or space that is not original to the house likely doesn't have the proper foundation to support another floor built above it. You'll most likely need the opinion of a structural engineer (and his or her fees) to answer this question.

4. *The most expensive way to build is out.* We've grown comfortable with the phrase "bump it out" to expand a room or add more space in a marginal way. If you are building on top of what is now dirt, it is the most expensive way to add space to your home. Any added space must sit atop either a concrete slab, a crawl space, or a basement, all of which require excavation and a visit from the cement truck, arguably the most expensive stand-alone component of the building process.

5. *The kind of space you add matters when it comes to cost.* Adding dry space that doesn't require plumbing is the least costly new space to add. Kitchens and bathrooms—which require plumbing, not to mention the juxtaposition of heating, cooling, and

energy such as gas lines—are the most expensive, per square foot, either to build new or to renovate.

6. While you're at it, it really is more efficient to go for it. There is a saying that starts like this: "While the cement truck is at your house, go as deep as you can." This

Recognizing the need is the primary condition for design.

—CHARLES EAMES

means that if you're building a first-floor addition, building over that addition will be less expensive if both floors are built at the same time. And certainly, building underneath it will also be cheaper. If you are already pouring a foundation for a first-floor addition, digging lower to create basement space underneath is worth doing if you can find the extra $5,000 to $10,000 at that point, if you have even the slightest need for additional space below your house.

7. You often won't live through an addition. You often can't live in your house when your roof is open to the elements. It's no picnic to live through a major renovation, but because additions create large holes in the existing envelope—as in the roof over your head—chances are you'll be forced to move into your basement, stay with relatives, or live in a hotel for a month or more, especially if you have children. Adults on their own can sometimes stomach wearing their winter coats to bed, using the neighbor's shower, eating each meal at the diner down the street, or all three. I have done all these things many times, testing my marriage greatly each time. I would not consider it even for a moment now that I have small children.

8. *You don't really know (anything) for sure until you demo.* You can have all kinds of structural engineering reviews and historical documentation about what might be behind your walls, but until the laborer carrying a hatchet starts to break them apart, nothing is certain. With newer homes, there is less mystery, but there are still surprises. With older homes, a lot can reside within the walls: old electrical or plumbing components, problems like mold or termites, imperfections in the structure or its integrity. There are almost always work-arounds—no one ever takes a wall down only to put it right back up because they found something unpleasant—but unforeseen surprises make for additional costs and delays.

I hope that wasn't all sobering news to the uninitiated. Just because it's expensive and challenging doesn't mean it's off the table, to be sure. But it does mean you should consider any and all possibilities within the envelope—that is, within the existing exterior walls—first. Consider how to make your kitchen bigger by merging the dining space with it, how to make the bathroom bigger by swallowing up the adjacent closet, how to enlarge your kids' bedroom by taking the closet out altogether and using an armoire, or how to eliminate an unused bedroom to make a better living room. Good design and small spaces are not odd bedfellows. Good design doesn't need a lot of space to work, just thoughtfulness and creativity.

If you have big problems with your home and feel an addition is the only option, take these three steps before you do anything else:

1. *Research the municipal zoning restrictions through your local planning department. Obtain a document called the plat, which is a bird's-eye view of your property and all its boundaries.*

2. *Get a short list of contractors from friends who've had good experiences. Listen to their addition stories carefully. Make sure their projects are fairly comparable to the scale and complexity of what you're interested in doing.*

3. *Sit down with your spouse or partner and talk honestly about spending a minimum of $50,000 (and probably much more, which is difficult and costly to finance) as well as enduring a great disruption to your daily life for months.*

After completing these steps, if you are still interested in an addition, you are ready to move forward: hiring a team, making plans for the work to begin, and deciding how you'll function once your house is a construction site. Take as much time as you need to prepare and even more time to hire the right person. Rarely does the full process happen, start to finish, in less than twelve months for substantial projects.

PUTTING IT ALL TOGETHER

A great home is a partnership between occupant and structure, expressed in a strong and soulful personal aesthetic. You've dug deep into your past, unearthing the fundamentals that you'll bring to design choices, walls, and how you will use your space. Your house is your partner—even if you don't think it's a great one—and it helps to recognize what it does offer, what can be played up, and how it can be improved realistically and respectfully. This is what we worked on in Parts One and Two. In Part Three, we take all the fundamental ingredients and figure out how to start merging you and your house. This is a bit more technical than introspective, although a lot of Part Three is about building your confidence. If you don't believe in yourself and feel inspired, not much happens.

How do you begin to express everything that makes up your life now in the home you have? And how do you make that work across the house in a way that feels good? How do you get and stay inspired? These are the topics we'll tackle next, as you begin to realize your strong, soulful, personal aesthetic.

The home should be the
treasure chest of living.

—LE CORBUSIER

18

FIND YOUR KERNEL

*Choose something meaningful
from your life to guide you in any
new design project.*

Are you starting over or anew with your entire house or just one
troublesome room? Either way, you need a kernel. Take something
you love, something that conjures memories and good feelings of
a particular time in your life, a particular relationship, or a place
in the world that you've visited, and make it your catalyst for
design in your space. It can be a decorative item, memento, book,
picture, or artwork. This is your *kernel*—the little seed that you can
draw from, build on, and tell a story with; it will lead you to the
answer for every design decision you face. Each space you work on
deserves its own unique kernel, or meaningful starting point. The
more specific and personal, the better.

When I designed my daughter's tiny attic bedroom, my
kernel was the cover of an old sewing pattern I found after my
grandmother, a master seamstress and serious collector of sewing
patterns, passed away. The well-worn paper cover showed a 1950s
fashion sketch of a woman in a navy-blue coatdress with a wide
ruffle from collar to hem. This kernel was anything but arbitrary
as a starting point for my daughter's nursery: I love the color navy
and anything vintage, I missed my grandmother, and for our first

girl after three sons, I wanted the room to be feminine, but not in a pink tutu kind of way.

The next move was to consider the space I was working with—its shape, size, era, and features. The kernel is the inspiration; your space is the palette. That pattern cover could have led me in a lot of different directions, but once I considered the space, I chose to play up the room's assets rather than dwell on its limitations. The deeply sloped ceiling and the lone window became focal points when I put up cream ruffled curtains at the window and applied a navy brocade pattern to the ceiling. It was easy to tease out colors and streamlined shapes that appealed to me from the pattern. My memory of my grandmother and my impressions of an era before my time filled in the blanks. Even though no one else would know, I think of my grandmother every time I walk into my daughter's room—her sewing, 1950s glamour, and the sumptuousness of a smart dress is right there with me.

Starting with a kernel is a creative action to allow something you love, something you're drawn to, to reverberate throughout the space. Rooms are complex places—furniture, flooring, window treatments, accessories, lighting, linens—and it can feel overwhelming to make choices. When you're confident in your starting point and are clear on why you like it so much, it's a lot easier. Letting something reverberate in your space means you pull the physical features out of something meaningful (in my case, ruffles, navy, and midcentury fashion), whether it's a place you've visited or a work of art you love, and allowing those features to guide the rest of what goes into the room.

When you've got your kernel, you can visualize what you want and not stand in front of a retailer's choices with a blank stare. Focusing on the features expressed in your kernel naturally narrows down your choices. You're after subtlety and nuance about what's meaningful to you, so the connection need not be screamed, just whispered. Themes scream things, as in "This is a beach house!" Sensibility is less specific, because it's personal. What says "beach" to me may not say "beach" to you, and this doesn't matter. You're not creating your house for me. If you do want to have a beach-house feel, think about what this means to you. What are your favorite aspects of your beach? A Ferris wheel and children screaming immediately come to mind for me and make me giddy (the Jersey in me). How about you? Red-painted toenails in warm sand? Your sun-kissed family playing poker around the table at the rental? Brightly colored beach umbrellas? The shiny hull of a boat? Cotton candy? Piping plovers? If you allow stores to fill the beach blank for you with generic beach stuff, you aren't finding that specificity that has an emotional tug, a nostalgic pull that makes a home feel really good—this is what a good personal starting point does for you.

Let's say you grew up in New Hampshire, and your kernel is a watercolor of a farmhouse amid full foliage from a local artist. You might make the following list of modifiers, drawn out of the art:

- *Reds, oranges, and gold*
- *Pewter and iron*
- *Rustic shapes*
- *Rough-hewn wood*
- *Weathered materials*
- *Organic shapes*
- *Clapboard*
- *Faux fur*
- *Simple patterns*
- *Stripes*

This is a good guide to take shopping. You may already have some things to start with that convey these items and descriptions. This is more about pulling out the textures, shapes, and attributes of your inspiration as opposed to obvious emblems or signage that seem to scream what you're drawing from. It doesn't need to be that obvious, and more will come from choosing the materials and qualities of what you love than from using literal images.

The stronger the feelings and more intense the response to your kernel, the more creatively powerful it will be for your space. Find your kernel and spend time really looking at it; note the colors, shapes, and textures. If your kernel is an experience or a faraway place instead of a discreet object, spend some time thinking about it. When you make the early decisions for your space out of love, putting your house together is more enjoyable. The answers just come, because you're not trying to mimic a magazine or apply some kind of design rules. You're starting from your own experience and memory and from shapes and textures you already love. When you limit yourself to what's important to you, the universe of overwhelming choices becomes more manageable. And when you let references from your awesome life guide you, your whole house will remind you of great things you've done, places you've been, or people you've loved. This is what creating lasting beauty is all about.

What is one object, piece of art, textile, photograph, knick-knack, or memory that you really love? Choose something that has a lot of significance to you. List five physical attributes of this object or concept: what colors, textures, fonts, time periods, shapes, feelings, urges, smells, and sounds do you associate with this object? This is your kernel for a space that needs a turnaround.

Don't rush this process. Your intention to make this room what you want is already on paper. You really don't need to look at someone else's interpretation of a room that conveys your kernel. However, if you want to see how specific elements might work together, that's a great way to use Pinterest, Google, or design blogs. You can plug the features or adjectives of your chosen kernel such as "fall colors" or "wrought iron" or "white washed wood" into Pinterest's home decor tab. This way, you use the Internet piecemeal rather than finding a room you love online and then trying to replicate someone else's choices. This is about going inward first, gathering your answers, and then using your available resources to make the room come together.

🏠 Creativity is just connecting things. When you ask creative people how they did something, they feel a little guilty because they didn't really do it, they just saw something. It seemed obvious to them after a while. That's because they were able to connect experiences they've had and synthesize new things.

—STEVE JOBS

19

CREATE A THROUGH LINE FOR THE WHOLE HOUSE

Pick a way to make your aesthetic cohesive throughout your house.

In the last chapter, you began to identify your aesthetic through inspiring and personal starting points, or kernels. What if your kernels are all over the place as you move from room to room? What if you're drawn to different things for different parts of your house? You may want to reference an African safari that held a great deal of significance for you in the living room but then give a nod to your Italian past in your kitchen. How can you do that without creating a home that feels disjointed, unconnected, and awkward? Without watering down what's important to you for the sake of making the house flow easily?

You want your story to reverberate throughout the whole house, and it's your aesthetic that will bind all the pieces together. Begin to notice what the things you love have in common, even those things and experiences from far-flung origins. It's not particularly difficult to have a cohesive house where all the spaces are unique but connected; however, this does take planning, thought, commitment, and most of all, *time*.

If you feel like you need some kind of grand plan or set of color or style rules for your house so everything goes together, it's not your fault. Magazines often show homes where each room is a dutiful soldier in some kind of color-coordinated army. We're told, "Simply use the same colors over and over again so the rooms bleed into one another and create a visual connection." So does that mean you must pick the same three colors and just reuse them in every space in your house? I've had clients apologize for their color choices, saying, "I went into left field here with this blue, but I got sick of the taupe theme in the other part of the house." Of course they did! We're told that things need to *coordinate*, another word I find ill-suited to a personal house. At this point, many people may feel like saying, "I'll just put the same style furniture in every room. Better yet, I'll buy all my furniture for my whole house at the same store so everything is coordinated!" The notion of each room having the same look and feel comes from some sort of retail-showroom-oriented design system. Leave *coordinated* to describe a person who can juggle while riding a bike—for your home, choose *connected* instead.

Go back to the work you did in Part One and consider your life's dominant chapters and characters. Is it your heritage? Your extensive travel? Your passion for cooking? Your large extended family? My grandparents and my husband's relatives loom large in our house because connecting to the past is important to me. I have their things, their pictures, and their art throughout my home. Travel, time at the beach, and humor are also important. I am drawn to nearly every shade of blue in the fan deck; you can tell as soon as you walk in my door. What things make up your aesthetic? It's your memories and what you're drawn to that builds this—not what's available in the marketplace.

You have choices about how you want to connect your spaces. If you are starting with empty rooms, you can pick one of the approaches that follow. If you are trying to work with what you already have, consider how you can add or remove to create patterns and commonalities throughout your space.

COLOR COHESION

I draw from a vast ocean, so to speak, of blues and greens. I use navy to denim to art deco mint; frothy sage to olive to robin's egg blue; highlighter green to sky blue to stormy gray. Don't be afraid to use the outer limits of each color that you love. If you are a red lover, don't be afraid to use the palest blush pink as well as race-car red and merlot, all with fabulous results. This is a way to connect space with color without it feeling like a straightjacket.

Using one color is like having a license to use its variant somewhere nearby; it sets the stage. You may choose a deep eggplant for your walls in one room, a pale shade of lavender for a chair in the adjacent room, and curtains with thin violet stripes in your kitchen. This is color connection—not all the same shade of purple, not purple splattered everywhere, but purple paired with whatever colors and textures suit each space.

Another key to using color as your cohesive factor is using "something out of left field" sparingly, like one of those spices you use at the end of a recipe to give a dish a distinctive flavor without dominating it. Perhaps you want a dash of navy blue or sunflower yellow in your pink-and-red room. Adding a touch of a contrast color can inject a little personality. Feel free to use a different spice in each room in your house, even if you use pink and red (or whatever your favorites are) in each space. My spice of femininity, whimsy, and countercoolness is sockeye salmon—an orangey pink that commands attention, even when used only sparingly in a sea of blues and greens.

SHAPE AND TEXTURE COHESION

You can also connect your spaces with things that have the same feeling or shape. If you are more drawn to textures or shapes than to color, this will work fabulously for you. Be careful not to go "themey" here. This is not about saying, "I love elephants," and letting elephants fill every blank space in your home, answering every question for pattern, artwork, and so on. This is about going to your list, seeing that nature, for example, is a big part of what you want your home to express or have inside it, and bringing the natural world in all its forms into each room.

If you are drawn to all things nature, this desire comes from time spent outdoors, most likely on hikes, at the beach, during walks, while camping or exploring. Draw from actual experiences using either things you've discovered yourself or new things. Don't be led by somebody else's "nature." Whether it's shells, plants, watery elements, rocks, unfinished wood, woven textures, flowers, animals, taxidermy, vintage botanical or biological textbooks or prints, feathers, nature photography, or something else that signifies nature to you personally, use it liberally in every room in your house. Don't be afraid, even in a small house, to go big here—if it's your thing, make it prominent—using oversized specimens or a series of fifteen botanical prints instead of three.

OBJECT COHESION

Perhaps there is something from your heritage, your geography, or your calling that you'd like to use as your connective tissue in every room or most rooms. For instance, something from your time abroad, your African roots, or your study of medicine. This works well with art and crafts from a specific part of the world. When an object is carried throughout a house, the walls and furniture are there to support the artifacts of your life; they're not the stars of the show.

If you have fallen in love with a particular craft from somewhere in the world—for example, Latin American textiles—this can be an extraordinary through line. Woven goods from women of Andean descent, from Peru, Bolivia, Chile, and Guatemala, are traditionally bold and expressive abstract designs with a liberal use of bright colors. You can use a different piece in each room, allowing each piece both to be your guide as to how to color the rest of the room and to connect all your spaces. You need not use them everywhere; even just a small reminder does the job. You may have an all-white bedroom with a single tapestry hung on the wall to frame and illuminate the space with color and story. So you need not clothe your bed, pillows, and drapes in the vibrancy of *huipiles*. With your story, a light touch is best. Your artifacts will say more with less competition.

Remember that each room can and will have wildly different functions, usage, and levels of formality and tidiness. So while you may have an intention of connecting the rooms in some way, don't overdo it—let each room develop its own character based on how it's used.

Many of you may be saying, "Why must my rooms all have something in common? What is all this about connective tissue? Can't they be separate entities?" Indeed! This step is for those of us who are drawn aesthetically to commonality in connected spaces. Some houses almost beg for some kind of connective tissue. Sometimes it's the home owner who wants it that way. I've worked in many homes—especially larger, older houses—where each room really is a surprise and can take on a completely independent character successfully. There is something enjoyable about cleaning the slate as you approach each room and treating each space like a separate work of art, without any kind of reference or reverence for anything else used elsewhere in the house. If you are putting yourself into each specific space in your home, chances are there will be a kindred spirit in each room, if not something that visually connects them.

Once again, for the cheap seats—this is your house, your self-expression, your creative work. It doesn't matter if no one else sees "it," the thing that connects all the spaces. Create your spaces in a way that pleases you—you are the curator and the most important observer. Do this over time. The best way to make them connect may not be obvious right away.

YOUR TURN

FIND YOUR FIVE

Go back to Part One and find your most meaningful five—the backbone of your personal aesthetic. This is a list of five things, concepts, places, experiences that express who you are and what you love. You can have your favorite places, artists, foods, fashion labels, or lazy Sunday activities on your list. From you list of five, tease out what attributes or adjectives logically follow—colors, shapes, textures. You are fleshing out, with words, your aesthetic and getting clearer on what to look for in the marketplace.

BLENDING STORIES

I've worked with clients who have so much story in their house, they feel lost in it. Tapestries from Southeast Asia, antiques from an English grandmother, nature photography from time spent in the Bay Area. When your life is so interesting and varied that you have this problem, don't worry. It will all come together, but you have to be picky. Take each piece and answer the following questions:

1   *Do you love it? Are you keeping it more because of fond memories than your love of the object? You need to love the story behind the object and the object itself for it to work in your house.*

2   *What is it that you love about this piece? Be descriptive.*

Hopefully this exercise will allow the common threads to reveal the most beloved artifacts of your life. Some things may seem to have no connection in provenance but do in their material features, as in, the color red or graceful curves. If you can find one feature that two or three prominent pieces in the room share, they will take center stage, working together as the dominant features in that room.

Birds are so much wiser than we! A robin builds a nest for robins. A seagull builds a nest for seagulls. They don't copy each other—or build themselves nests as described in The Birds' Decorating Magazine.

—DOROTHY DRAPER,
IN THE PINK

20

BACK ONLINE, BACK TO MAGAZINES

*Selectively engage with design media
to learn, curate your ideas, and find
out the "how."*

From the work we've done so far, you have answered the question "What should I put in my house?" It's all there. With that groundwork laid, now is a good time to go back to blogs and house-themed social media to look for the *how.* As in, "How should I compose a mantel with my dad's old lacrosse sticks?" Or, "How can I display my collection of African masks in a fresh way?" The images on Pinterest and Houzz are great for learning methods and adapting ideas into which you can insert your narrative. If you come to these tools confident in what you want to fill your house with, you won't be tantalized by what other people have done to express their lives, which may be very different from yours.

Design media is so entertaining. For lots of people, myself included, it's tantalizing to look at other people's houses, especially the truly fabulous ones. It's also fun to see the crafty among us show all kinds of things we can make out of other things—old doors become headboards, quilts become poufs, pallets become walls. This is what our media world allows us to experience every minute of the day: other people's creativity all the time. If your objective is to get clear on what your house needs for you to love it and get your own creative power going, this is not going to help you. There are also problems inherent in looking at home design: you can't get the whole picture in any one photo, and you certainly can't get the experience of being there.

Houses are messy places where all our personal business takes place, and they hold everything from piles of bills to dirty bathrooms. Magazine spreads never show this, so you are seeing something far removed from what a home looks like in real life. Like the blemishes on a model's face, the realities of life are always removed from view. Certainly messy homes don't sell magazines or get pinned much, but photos of perfectly coifed rooms raise our expectations—or at least the aspirations most of us have for our homes. Not to mention, these photos don't tell the real story of where the mail, dirty laundry, and kid stuff are.

Go back to your media mistresses carefully. When you look at a house in a magazine or online, do so with a critical, if not skeptical, eye. You also have to remember how you live. That's why it's so important to be clear on not only who you are but how you live, so you can evaluate a photograph or project and determine whether or not it can be helpful to you. When you're looking at photographs for a specific project, try to find images that have a lot in common with your situation.

Process is mostly absent from design magazines. There is little explanation of how a room came to be: where things were purchased; how paint was selected; what paint was selected; how built-ins were made; why ceilings were or were not vaulted; when windows were replaced, enlarged, or moved. Not only is process as a whole absent, but the why part of process is also missing—what the residents needed or wanted that led them to the changes now worthy of a glossy magazine spread. To be fair, furniture sources are listed for some spreads, but how rooms are composed is a complex story. A designer frequently takes credit for an entire room. In my experience, this is seldom accurate. More often, it's the work of many.

If you see a house or project that truly inspires you, it's worth exploring how that room came to be: how old it is, who built it, and where the elements you really appreciate came from. Contact the publisher or the designer and ask questions. Make the still image come to life to help you understand how the room was achieved and how things might be replicated in your home. This is a much more active process than sticking the photos inside a dream file, and thus more productive in helping you use those images for your own house.

MAKE SURE THE SPACE MATCHES

If you are looking at kitchens online or in magazines, make sure you are looking at kitchens that are roughly the same size as yours. This seems obvious, but people often fall in love with the look and feel of a room without realizing how the elements will work with their space allotment. This can go either way: if your kitchen is large, you'll typically need a lot more cabinetry, flooring, and countertops than someone whose kitchen is small. So don't fall in love with a surface displayed in a small, sunlit galley kitchen; it will look very different in a larger space with less light.

It's helpful to bring your house along for this ride. When you're doing your visual searches, keep your photos beside you. I prefer printed photographs sitting on my desk as I leaf through magazines or page through pictures online, but you can also use digital photos. If you drew a floor plan of your home, have that on hand too. You constantly want to remind yourself of what you're working with. Even if you are changing the space dramatically, you should still keep your home as a point of reference. And if you're trying to work with lots of existing furniture or fixtures, by all means, keep photos of what you're working with handy. The constant mental reference of your space in the abstract, the strain to think how things will look, is exhausting, so make it easy on yourself. Bring your computer or tablet into the space you're working on or keep your photos beside the computer.

CHOOSE YOUR MEDIA SOURCES WISELY

Don't limit yourself based on style. There are certainly magazines (such as *Dwell*) that have a pattern of exclusively showing more contemporary-styled spaces, while others (such as *Veranda*) focus on more ornate, feminine, complicated, and "traditional" rooms. But don't limit yourself based on their reputation or brand. Most magazines that aim to appeal to a wide audience try to provide a variety of different spaces. If anything, limit what you look at based on scale. Because we are not using the "traditional" or "modern" style monikers, do searches for spaces based on size and light, and look at everything that comes up. If you have a small powder room and you know you want it to be a bright color, you might do a search for "small powder rooms with jewel-toned walls" on Houzz or Pinterest. This way you won't be limited to how one person defines modern or traditional.

By being selective and disciplined with magazine and online images, I'm hoping to help you avoid more than just a monumental waste of your time—it's actually worse than that. The bigger problem is when people fall in love with entryways that have no relationship to what they are working with. Or when they become inspired by projects that are not feasible based on the parameters (space, budget, lighting, climate, and so on) they have. This process is not intended to be a big magazine buzzkill but to give you a way to make the publications work for you. Think of them as a possible research tool: it's your job to find the pictures and sources that are applicable and to *let the rest go*. You can always go back to the eye-candy version of magazine consumption and just look for fun, but when you're trying to make your home better and create a space that reflects who you are, it's more about eye *salad* and using images that are good for you and your house journey.

YOUR TURN
FRUITFUL SEARCHES

Keep these rules in mind to have more fruitful searches when you're problem solving a design issue in your house:

1. *Set a time limit and be focused.* When you're working on space and drawing inspiration from other people's houses, don't endlessly look online or in magazines. Designate the time you spend in front of design media based on your intentions and a time limit.

2. *Ask specific questions.* If you are trying to solve the issue of an entryway that isn't working for you, you'll need to have a photograph of your own foyer or entryway on hand for reference, with measurements. Make specific searches through either Google,

Houzz, or Pinterest based on the ideas you are gathering. Do you want a more organized entryway for kid stuff? Do you want a place to showcase art or something soothing to greet you? Do you want to do something dramatic with color? These kinds of questions lead you to more fruitful searches. As I was writing this, I typed "pretty entryways" into Houzz and got more than sixty thousand results. Even if you could review them all, 98 percent wouldn't be useful or applicable. The key is to make targeted, specific searches and to complement your image searches with examples you find in your built environment—in the homes of friends or neighbors.

3. *Rip it out and tape it up.* What do you do with images you've fallen in love with? Don't stick them in a file somewhere. Rip them out or print them out, and tape them to the wall of the room you intend to work on. Pinterest boards are great, but how likely are you to revisit the photos and dissect what they can offer you if they are buried in the Pinterest vortex? If they're going to help you, you need to look at these images and be surrounded by them as you casually walk by. Perhaps you've snipped images of furniture, whole rooms, or beautiful images from nature—whatever you've collected, put them up on your walls. In chapter 9, you created a treasure map of images that you found attractive for your home. That was a way of finding out what appeals to you and stirring up desires or preferences on paper, sort of a journal entry in pictures. Now bring those images into your home, quite literally, to see what's applicable to your space, to see if you can start a project that works for you, and to get comfortable with how the new space will be.

21

FIND YOUR PEOPLE

*Carefully compile a creative council and
gather ideas from the houses around you.*

It's a natural human desire to connect with others during a creative
process—whether it's about choosing a paint color or deciding
how to use a particular space—for feedback or to talk through
the process of finding a solution. People I know with the most
beautiful homes usually have creative friends who are happy to
come over and talk through a change that's being considered or
help rearrange the furniture. While it can be wonderful to employ
a professional designer, what is often missing (but essential) in a
professional relationship is the kinship and familiarity of a close
friend who knows you and your family.

Some of what our friends and family have to say about our
house is useful, some is not. Too often we listen to criticism about
our home that isn't supportive. We tend to open ourselves up
when we start expressing our disappointment with our home. We
are likely to get some "what you should really do in here is" style
rants from people in our lives who already know all the answers.
These are the friends and family members who likely read thirty
home magazines a month and pay close attention to what *they*
like and what will work in *their* homes. But that doesn't necessarily
qualify them to help you with *your* house. When criticism comes

from your parents and/or in-laws, it can be even harder. Common intergenerational utterances like "This house is a bit tight," or "The living room could use some sprucing up, couldn't it?" often get translated in our minds to "This house and where you are in your life aren't good enough, and you aren't talented/grown up/adult enough to make your living room beautiful." The chasm between what someone else says and what happens when we translate it into something more dramatic is not anyone else's fault. For most of us, our home is a sensitive topic.

Seek out people who are supportive *and* knowledgeable when it comes to talking about your house. It's fine if your friends have great taste or a beautiful home of their own, but this doesn't mean they can help you. They can help you if they know you well, respect you, and have the time. If they are truly interested in helping you manifest what you want for your home—versus what they have or what magazines are displaying this season—they are great creative allies.

I come to this step honestly, having made many design decisions based on the feedback of others because I put them on a pedestal or took their comments too seriously. I find it almost too hard to shield myself from others' opinions. You can tell yourself, "This is only for me" a thousand times, but it's still hard to turn off the house committee in your head. A better strategy is to defend yourself from people who will never love what you're trying to do in your home and actively seek the feedback from the right people in your life. It's time to ditch the bitchy committee and instead put together a supportive creative council. Focus on people who know you and support you in other ways, rather than on people who seem to have a lot of design savvy, but not so much nice. People who know you and your story will support your choices. They'll appreciate seeing things from your life or things that have a connection to you. They will think of ways to incorporate your story because they know a bit of it. Someone has to be able to set aside what they would do or prefer or what makes *them* happy to work on your house.

YOUR TURN
HOW TO CHOOSE YOUR CREATIVE COUNCIL

1. *Choose people who are confident.* Confidence goes a long way in making a house beautiful. A confident friend will encourage you to trust yourself to take chances and not be afraid. He or she will remind you that a wrong paint color or even a wrong furniture purchase will not end your life. Can you think of one or two house-confident friends or relatives?

2. *Choose people who are interested.* Your creative council should include people who like the idea of making your house better for you. They should have an interest in interiors and all that goes into making a house better for daily life. They should never fault you for wanting to make your house great, thinking about it too much, or worrying about it too often. You may do all of these things, but someone who calls you on it is not a great creative ally. Your allies should enjoy the process of making a home great, not see it as an

> Criticism, like rain, should be gentle enough to nourish a man's growth without destroying his roots.
>
> —FRANK A. CLARK

annoying task to get done and check off their list. Who in your life is interested, even passionate, about all things home? He or she could be a great candidate.

3. Choose people who are kind. There is a place for that friend who calls it like it is. Your creative council isn't that place. The woman who gives her unvarnished opinion, her unedited feedback? Not the best creative ally. Seek out people who speak up honestly but can communicate in a supportive way. For example, you ask your creative council member, "Is this green too bright for my living room?" A good creative ally will say, "It might be. Let's look at others together," or, "What do you think?" Someone who is not a good creative ally will say, "Absolutely! Give me my sunglasses! What were you thinking?" Do you have someone nice in mind to help you?

4. Choose people who won't forget it's about you, not them, not trends, not what anyone else thinks, not solely about resale value. People with their own paranoia about resale value are the worst candidates for your creative council. Each family has a different real estate position, and anyone who comes in and asserts that they know what you should do based on their knowledge—whether it's from reading the real estate section of the newspaper religiously or based on their friend's-cousin-who's-a-top-salesperson—doesn't

know your story. I remember telling a friend that I wanted to add a garage and a big addition to my house, but I wasn't sure if it was worth it given that, in our neighborhood, houses weren't appreciating very much. This was when Washington, DC, was just climbing out of the downturn. Without hearing about why we might add on, why we were averse to moving, and not knowing me well enough to understand how much I'd thoroughly enjoy just about any renovation project I could possibly make happen, my friend said rather assertively, "No, you shouldn't do any of that. You won't get your money back. Just move." We had just moved into our house; in fact, as this conversation took place, we were standing amid boxes. It's not that her advice didn't make logical sense or even that it was wrong, but unless someone knows the whole story and has the patience to hear it as it evolves, their opinion can't really help.

Are there names that popped up again and again when you read these guidelines? Invite those people over for whatever you may all like to eat or drink and engage in house talk. Just because they are your creative council, it doesn't mean you do everything they say. Make a note of the good ideas that appeal to you, and be clear with your friends about your objectives: Tell them: "I want to make my dining room more dramatic and bold and more connected to my time in Spain." Don't ask them how to make it better unless the question is, "How can I make this room more me?" This works great when you can be a creative ally to someone else—have an exchange and take turns on whose house is the focus.

De gustibus non est disputandum. (Latin for "In matters of taste there can be no dispute.")

—FRANK RIENZO

22

ALL TOGETHER NOW

Working on the house with your beloved
takes a bit of design diplomacy.

Remember the introduction to MTV's *Real World*, the granddaddy
of all reality shows and the first to film perfect strangers living
together? It started with, "This is the true story of what happens
. . . when people stop being polite and start getting real!" Even
though you probably don't have a film crew in your house, living
with another adult (of your choosing) is often a challenge for the
easiest-going person.

I have had many awkward design consultations in the homes
of couples who want to tear each other's eyes out because they
can't agree on how to redo the kitchen, which paint to choose
for the living room, or even if they need me. We bring our own
experiences, preferences, and aesthetic to any relationship. Our
beloved might admire some of what we bring; it's likely he or she
can't stand other parts. One partner's ideas may feel like an assault
on the other's vision for the house. Whatever level of domestic
discord your relationship is experiencing in reference to how your
home is to be made, just know this is common. What helps good
spousal codesign is diplomacy.

What do you do if you are disgusted or just plain unamused
with your partner's ideas or preferences? Are you in the middle of

the classic gender-based aesthetic clash—he wants something dark, austere, and masculine, calling it modern; she wants something light, airy, and romantic and calls it traditional? It's usually more nuanced or complicated than that; couples often disagree on how a room should be used, who'll use it more, who pays for changes, who was here first, or just whose house it is, damn it. Often what seems like a desire for a leather couch or a pink wall is a layer cake of emotion and built-up frustration. Try to find out what else is there.

Here are some rules to make working together on your house easier and to protect the relationship that is the likely reason for the house in the first place.

1. *A home is a home to all and should welcome, soothe, and speak to everyone who lives there.* Everyone must be represented in the house. You don't want either partner feeling like a visitor or that the environment is not made for him or her. Often people get too focused on what style or furniture he likes versus what she likes. Switch the focus from style to story. Make sure both stories are told and that the lives, passions, travels, and interests before and after you became a "we" are imbued in the space. This enables everyone to feel comfortable. How can you put what you love about the other person into the space? Back away from strict personal preferences and work toward pieces and choices that have something to do with what makes your partner so lovable to you. When both of your stories, in addition to your collective story, are told in the house, both of you feel taken care of.

2. *Compose a mission together.* This is so important, and probably the last thing at least one of you wants to do. But it helps when you're both sitting on opposite sides of Crate & Barrel in very

different chairs, refusing to give an inch in the other direction. Or worse yet, when one of you won't even go to the store, then hates what the other one picks and insists it be returned. Been there, done that. A jointly penned mission solves this. It's not going to ensure that all decisions will go smoothly, but it will help you both define what you want out of your house—or even just a particular room—together. A two-sentence description of what the room would be like and do for you is all you need. Some people prefer bullet points to describe the room. Remember to be as descriptive as possible and not to use tired, hard-to-pin-down words like *warm* or *modern*. Try to bring in concrete examples of your story, as in "The living room will showcase Bob's love of nature and Ann's love of contemporary art, in balance, and it will be a restful place for us to read, watch TV together, talk, or have a glass of wine with friends on weekends."

Even though this alone can be a daunting goal, it can be done, and you lay the groundwork when everyone understands what's important to the other party right from the beginning.

3. *There is compromise and balance in everything.* My husband has a favorite photograph from his early twenties. He's pictured with his two uncles, young and effervescent, ecstatic to be on top of a mountain. You can read it on his face. I have hated this photograph since I first laid eyes on it. I am not particularly drawn to hiking or the outdoors. The magic of the mountaintop is lost on me, I know. Worse yet, I don't like the look of this photo—it is not properly edited or framed—and for a long time, it was these aesthetic hang-ups that blinded me to the sheer beauty and importance of this photograph to my husband. For years, it lived in our basement. Then one day, Francis retrieved it to show someone

who was visiting, and he became quite moved as he looked at it again. He so loves the men in this picture and that moment. It was such a big part of his story. I finally got it. It needed to be in our house, not under it. We hung it immediately, although I do have plans to frame it in a way I prefer someday.

Strong positive feelings need a big vote. If one party feels strongly about doing something, the other party can choose some way to be represented in the decision, but the strong feeling needs to be honored. If he must have leather couches, she can help choose them. If she must have green walls, he gets to make the final choice of which green they use. It is lovely to work together on creating spaces and putting both people into the choices. This is what makes a unified home. Yes, it takes a lot more time and negotiation, but the good news is that the couch or fixture or paint color that you both can love is out there. Just keep looking, talking, and trying. It is most definitely not done in a weekend and possibly not even in a calendar year. Beauty takes a long time.

4. *Don't merge preferences—balance them.* If you truly are sitting on opposite sides with wildly different aesthetic preferences for furniture or fixtures, don't try to find a middle ground and water down each other's choices. Try to balance them out. If one party wants a super curvy Chesterfield sofa, full of rolling curves and tufted softness, perhaps the other party, who wanted the streamlined stripped-down contemporary couch, can find a simple, straight-edged coffee table or chair to work beside it. (This is what a Chesterfield needs anyway.) It's more than fine to blend furniture preferences, creating a blended aesthetic. Both sides give in, both sides get to win, the room is balanced and more interesting. This is more about bringing in a range of textures and shapes than adhering to a style like glue. There is an old saying, "Would you rather be married or right?" Would you rather enjoy living with your spouse or get to pick out all the furniture yourself?

5. *Share the decision making and aesthetic building for the majority of the house, but if possible, provide each person with one space that is truly theirs.* You're going to have to work together on the rest of the house, but go ahead and have a man cave or a lady lair. Give each partner a space where he or she makes the majority of the decisions.

6. *Every paying party gets a vote.* If you hire a design professional, chances are one person will be in contact with that person more frequently than the other regarding the professional's proposals for new furniture, layout, color, and fixtures. It's essential that each spouse get a full vote and the designer's proposals be taken under advisement, together. One spouse will often try to use a professional's expertise as a way to outvote his or her other half. This breeds resentment and hostility. You don't want one person thinking angry thoughts every time he or she passes the living room because of being outvoted by someone who is long gone and left a bill. If one party doesn't like something and feels strongly about it, the designer has to go back to the well for more choices. Be firm on this. Designers often want to discount or discredit the vote of a dissenting party. Remember that the designer is not paying for it, both of you are. Good designers or architects will offer new ideas to accommodate any concerns from either partner or a respectful explanation of why they don't agree.

7. *If you are truly stymied, move on.* At times, two people come to a design standstill. There is no moving either party. She wants this, he wants that. There is no way to bridge the divide. Do not be tempted to bring in a tiebreaker. Simply move on to another project on which you'll have an easier time agreeing. Get some wins under your marital belts: choose things together that work for both of you and come back to the stand-off project after you've had some time to work on something positive together. Many times a project that seems too hard to figure out will look different after a two-week break.

8. *Make a budget accord.* Money is often behind the acrimony in decisions that seem like they are about couches or where to put a sink. It's essential that both partners form a united front on budget, especially when working with professionals. Find a number that works and stick with it. If you are uncomfortable with the budget, speak up and don't expect anyone to read your mind. The bigger the project, the longer and more involved the budget conversation should be. When spending money on your house, you're taking many factors into account, some of which you can only speculate on, such as "How will this affect the value of our home?" Others should be figured out concretely, as in "How shall we pay for this?" If you are the spouse advocating a bigger spend, make a case for it: that it can be accomplished, that it has some reasonable likelihood of increasing the value of your home based on real data, and last, *that it is important to you.* The last piece is the most important in budget consideration. If you want to spend money, don't make it about the real estate market or finding a good deal or someone else's opinion. Tell your partner that you want it and that it will

make you happy. This is more honest and concrete and much harder to argue with.

9. *If one spouse truly abdicates his or her role as codesigner and decision maker, keep him or her informed anyway.* It's not uncommon for one party to say, "I don't care. Do want you want." Never ever believe this. It's often men who claim they don't care. This may be true, but there is always something someone who says this cares about. Continue to keep your partner involved, and get his feedback on how things feel or how they are working. Men can sometimes reject the importance of aesthetics, but they'll rarely reject the importance of comfort. It's the job of both partners to accomplish both.

My husband appears not to be fully engaged about how something will look in our home when it's an abstract idea, but he is full of feedback—usually but not always positive—once something is under way or completed. I know that he cares very much about how something functions, how long it will last, how much maintenance it will require, and how every piece we purchase or project we undertake will affect our comfort level. So while he may not care to be intimately involved in the sourcing, planning, or designing of a particular project, I take his considerations by proxy. It took us a long time to purchase dining room chairs. While he didn't care about color, material, or scale, he cared a lot that the chairs be comfortable and sturdy for both our large bodies and our boys' considerable activity level at dinner. After we picked out our chairs at Basset Furniture, we were told that our choice is "very popular with men." The chairs were not my first choice, but I did order them in navy blue, and I have fallen in love with them. The fact that I have a comfortable husband at dinnertime with no cares or worries—at least about the chairs—is worth relinquishing my first (several) aesthetic choices. In my house, how things work and people's happiness are incorporated into the overall success of the room.

YOUR TURN

WORKING WITH YOUR BETTER HALF—GOT A PROBLEM?

Let's say you have a problem. You can't agree on what to do with the "extra room," a paint color, how to furnish the den, or whether to get a wall oven.

1   *The first step is being clear about the purpose of the space you're working on. The way to do that is to write a mission. What is the space, object, appliance, furniture, or color going to do in your home? What are your expectations of the room/ wall color/purchase? What does your partner expect?*

2   Next, each spouse should spend a little time online and find
    pictures of things connected to the project that appeal to him
    or her. Choose whatever site you like. Find five pictures that
    show something you like for the problem you're working with—
    whether it's a new couch, a paint color, or kitchen appliances.

3   Then, each spouse has to sell it. Come up with three or four
    attributes that justify why your choices are so great. I have
    learned the most from this last exercise. Each spouse should
    also come up with five attributes he or she doesn't like about
    the other partner's findings, if they are truly objectionable.

You will learn a lot from this exercise, and most likely each party will
soften somewhat. You'll find a way to meet expectations or intensions,
even if you don't know exactly what you want. You'll get the feeling
that you're in this together. All of this is constructive diplomacy and
classic negotiation that happens for any design problem. It's not the
worst idea to do your first few exercises over a glass of wine.

Home wasn't built in a day.

—JANE SHERWOOD ACE

23

SLOW IS THE ONLY WAY TO GO

Get acquainted with a healthy, thoughtful,
sometimes painfully slow pace of change.

I get antsy when my home isn't the way I want it to be. I want
things done yesterday. I want that sweet serenity of sitting in a
freshly minted space, adapted to what I need, filled with things
I want to live with and see every day. I don't want to wait—ever.
But wait I must. So much is gained when we breathe through the
home-building process and exercise patience, both when we have
to (you're renovating and the contractor is tied up, your furniture is
on back order, you're saving up) and when we don't. It's tempting
to dive in to a project and make it happen. But I have had the best
results when I've waited, forced myself to slow down, and slept on
many a design decision.

The pace of most home improvements is relatively slow. Most
of us have little time to spend on our spaces, given the demands
of family and work outside the home. Then there are the physical
limitations. The work on your home is physical labor, and unless
you're in your early twenties, you probably don't have ten hours of
manual labor in you without taking away from some other demand
on your energy. Even projects that seem small can take a long time.
It's simple math: the more people, materials, and square footage
involved, the longer it's going to take. Hanging a framed work of

art is relatively simple—it doesn't take up much space or require many tools. Anything more than that, as well as the addition of tools, space affected, and the possibility of something going wrong, means that home improvements just take a long time.

The physical labor is rarely to blame for how long something takes. It's usually us, the home owners, who can't make a decision or who worry too much about making a mistake. Think about how long it takes most people to hang art on their walls. It's not nailing something into a wall that's hard—it's making a choice and committing to looking at something, at least for a while. This is not criticism; anything in your home demands thought and careful consideration.

More complicated home renovations and improvement projects make for complex choreography in finding, hiring, and managing tradespeople; acquiring materials; navigating nonworking days on the calendar—not to mention your own decision-making process. And in the production that is a complicated renovation project, the most important dance number is still your ability to decide what you want.

I have been accused of changing my mind often with contractors, carpenters, and other tradespeople. It's annoying to people charged with doing the work and finishing it on time, when I have a stroke of genius midstream. I try hard not to change my mind after the work starts, but sometimes the thinking isn't finished and the work has already begun. I also know that with some tradespeople who are eager to complete work before I'm ready, I need to slow things down, think through the project more thoroughly, and do my work before anyone shows up.

Slowing down makes for a more complete process. You'll have time to consider your project, what will happen to it, or how you'll need it to be for a host of circumstances. For example, if you're designing a child's room, take time to think through the maturity of the child—what happens in five years? What happens when your son's shoes are twice the size? When he is twice the height? When he needs a place for homework? Where will blankets be stored in winter? Will there be enough light to read to your daughter? For her to read on her own?

Slowness doesn't work with deadlines. How many times have I heard that a client wants to do something "before the holidays"? The pressure of accomplishing something before a big family party, the arrival of overnight guests, someone's graduation party, or the birth of a baby will most certainly cause you to compromise something in your design process. Plus, the stress on your daily life that is a home improvement project, even one as simple as a paint job, is even more intense with a holiday deadline. I have made this mistake many times, squeezing in some interesting "little" project before a party. There is nothing like hosting to inspire you to do the thing you've been wanting to do for a while. But home projects don't get squeezed in elegantly. You'll add undue stress, pay more, and end up with a less satisfactory result when you have to finish something because of an upcoming event. The best position to be in is indifferent about when something gets done.

One of my father-in-law Frank's favorite phrases is, "Slow and steady wins the race." If the race trophy is having a house you love and getting there affordably with as few regrets and unnecessary cash outlays as possible, this couldn't be more true. I am a fan of balancing the quick wins and letting the bigger projects simmer on the stove, which means I am willing to paint a room that may get gutted in a year, rather than leave it untouched and hate it every day until it gets done. If you would rather not put money into something that will get demolished, that is your choice, and go with it! You are more patient and probably more mature than I am. I need to make space mine in a small way, even if I'm planning on making it mine in a big way somewhere down the road. Once again, this is about knowing yourself and what you can live with—two things no one else can tell you.

YOUR TURN

WHAT'S YOUR TIMING?

Manage your expectations for home improvement. Understanding the following unofficial timelines will give you some advance warning and perspective.

1. *Did you just move in? It takes six months to move in to a new house.* You might be sleeping in your own bed the first night you arrive, but to actually move in and find a space for everything, getting your bearings in a new space—not to mention making any improvements—takes six months. It takes five years of diligent work to really make it yours—not finish it—but feel like yours.

2. Did you just get a bid from someone to do some work? Double any timetable the contractor or design professional provided. This does not mean design pros or contractors lie or are incapable of forecasting their own deadlines. But they are often giving you a time frame for your project, independent of all the other things that could possibly slow it down. That means if your bathroom had been remodeled in a vacuum, it could have taken two weeks. But because the tile guy got sick, the toilet is on back order, the company's previous job called the team back for two days, and the whole thing happened over the Fourth of July holiday, it actually took a month.

3. Are you plotting a large-scale addition? Live in your house for a full set of seasonal changes before making any big renovations or additions. It takes time to see what a house is like throughout the year. I suppose if you live in a temperate climate, which I have never done, and the weather is fairly consistent, you don't need to wait a whole year. But you don't lose anything from waiting and taking your time. Most homes are sold in spring and summer and moved into in late summer and early fall. This means that winter is an unknown experience, with leaves off the trees and less daylight that may affect how you make changes to your house or how you address certain rooms.

4. Are you trying to prioritize everything you want done now? Do one thing at a time. In a house with lots of problems and challenges, it's tempting to have multiple projects going at once. If you are gutting the entire house and have experience with this process, it is not really possible to do things piecemeal. But if you can, take your time and focus on one space at a time. Each project needs your full attention.

Part Four

ROOM-BY-ROOM BASICS

Do you want to redo every square inch of your home? Or do you have a few problem areas? Maybe you simply want more of your story and who you are infused into your house. This section will approach common problems, offering basic design philosophy and techniques, with a focus on putting what's best for you and your family into your space. If you have created a priority list, feel free to skip to the sections that apply to what you're going to work on first.

For the biggies—kitchens and baths—I merely scratch the surface, and this is intentional. I could never cover kitchen design in one chapter, and maybe not even one book. However, the surface, so to speak, is how kitchens that are boring can become personal. Bathrooms are the same; they are costly and painful to renovate but can often be tweaked and modified inexpensively to become interesting and expressive.

I think you'll find that personalizing other rooms in the house, such as the bedroom, are also straightforward endeavors and can be extremely rewarding to your daily life. However you start, big or small, simple or complex, the questions are the same: What do you need from this room every day? What story are you telling? How can you put more of yourself here?

24

WELCOME YOURSELF HOME: ENTRYWAYS

*Create an entryway that suits your needs
and truly welcomes you or anyone else.*

Most of us want our homes to be welcoming. Welcoming to whom? Rather than focus solely on the experience of your visitors, think about how you might welcome *yourself* home, as well as how you might send yourself off in a thoughtful way. This is the purpose of entryways: to embrace us on arrival; transition us and our things from "out there" to "in here"; and when it's time, to send us off again feeling ready and organized.

It's tough to think about aesthetics for such hardworking spaces. We like to envision the kind of entryways we see on soap operas—a large, open foyer that's neat as a pin, with nary a coat or shopping bag in view, and centered by a large table brimming with fresh-cut flowers. Actors and actresses saunter by, presumably after a servant has taken their coats, and the entryway serves as little more than a pretty space to walk through. I don't know about you, but that couldn't be further from my truth. My entryway is part bus terminal, part mailroom: there are people coming, going, and waiting; mail and boxes at times stacked child-high. A hardworking and accommodating entryway is a tall order, with or without servants. A welcoming entryway, one that makes you smile or feel happy to have arrived, is even harder to achieve but such a nice gift to give yourself.

A smile is the universal welcome.

—MAX EASTMAN

Home owners can often realize one (make it attractive and welcoming) or the other (accommodate armloads of outerwear or mail) but not both. Although achieving both is tricky, it will make you happy. Assuming your home does not offer soap opera–scale architecture and you have a relatively small space with which to work (the most common entryway dilemma), let's review what every well-functioning entryway needs at its most basic level. These are not in any particular order of importance.

DEFINE THE SPACE

Entryways in older homes rarely accommodate the complexity of modern life and all of our stuff. If I had a dime for every time I heard a mother of school-aged children say, "I need a mudroom so badly," or a nickel for every time I've heard someone in an older home say, "In my house, we walk right into the living room," I'd be on a beach somewhere. If you're working with the space you have and adding more space is not in the cards, at least for the moment, do not shoehorn an entryway function into a room that's already chock-full. Don't hang a hook on the wall with a floor mat below and say, "This is where I put my stuff when I come in," unless you are extraordinarily neat and tidy, live alone, and enjoy an environment that allows you to wear flip-flops year-round. Instead, devote a *substantial* space to all the things either you or your guests may need when entering and leaving your house, even if this means compromising living space.

There are the obvious needs—a place for keys and mail, a place to hang a coat per person, a place on or near the floor for shoes. Then there are the less obvious, or only obvious when they are missing, such as the seat for putting on shoes, the space for outgoing shopping bags or gifts, and places for seasonal items like beach towels or mittens. A good rule of thumb is to give each occupant a place for all his or her things throughout the year. Perhaps the swimming-bag spot and the winter-hats-and-gloves spot are interchangeable. Keep it organized by going preschool: give everyone their own cubbies, hooks, and bins. Be generous, and give each person in the space ample room to get dressed and gather belongings, as well as get undressed and put away belongings. Make it attractive with bins and boxes you enjoy looking at—they can be rattan, Lucite, aluminum, wood, or whatever you like—and it won't seem like you're encroaching on your living space undesirably. Know yourself well enough to determine whether you'd prefer to look at your stuff out on hooks or put it all behind the closed door of a closet or an accommodating piece of furniture with cubbies and drawers.

Use the whole height of your walls, and choose an interesting area rug to define the entryway and corral outside dirt. In our house, I opened up the back wall of a closet that previously served our adjacent TV room. Now that old closet serves the entryway as an open mudroom of sorts. I closed the original opening up, losing the closet and its original purpose. I willingly robbed Peter to pay Paul by doing this, but I would much rather have order in the comings and goings with four children than give up the random-stuff closet that, as it was, was tucked away and not useful.

Because I could use space from another room, I have an architecturally defined and ample-sized area for all the stuff that needs to go out and much of the stuff we bring in (such as backpacks, boots, and the like). If you can't do this, the simplest option for a functional entryway is a series of hooks, a simple but ample bench, good-sized bins underneath the bench for shoes, and some kind of shelf or surface big enough for a few sets of keys and a big mail day. Paint the wall behind the bench a different color, put an area rug on the ground, and don't crowd yourself—this is an area that probably gets used multiple times a day.

THE LANDING STRIP

The term *landing strip*, which I did not coin (Maxwell Ryan, the founder and CEO of Apartment Therapy, did), describes a functional area for sorting and keeping mail, keys, and anything else that comes in the door. It's where everything incoming has a place to land. It could also be called the *departure strip*, a term I did coin, to describe a place that holds stuff until you need to leave again (outgoing mail, shopping bags, library books, wallet, keys, and so on). This is the space that can overwhelm houses—piles of mail and unread newspapers, outgoing mail, or stuff to be recycled. This is where you'll need a system and the daily discipline to keep it tidy. If you're someone who can go through things daily and purge unwanted flyers then and there, have a bin for junk mail. If you're someone who wants to put things somewhere and deal with them later (that would be me), have a place for items to be read and sorted that is big enough to hold a week's worth of mail.

Get Hooked

When searching for coat hooks, get more than you need—and for heaven's sake, get ones you love to look at. As you shop, look well beyond anything called a coat hook; nearly anything that protrudes from the wall a good one to two inches can be used as a hook in an interesting way. Put them at various heights. If you have more than you need, you get to look at a few bare hooks, even on the worst wintery days with the most people inside. This is a good thing.

LET THERE BE LIGHT

Light is often overlooked in the entryway. Some people think, *I have an overhead light, and there is light elsewhere in the room, so I'm fine.* Adding some kind of light devoted purely to the entryway helps quite a bit with all the arriving, depositing, readying, and leaving activities. Ideally, you need a task light and an overhead light. If you are really short on space and can't fit or afford a piece of furniture to act as a tabletop for a lamp, keep in mind that plug-in wall sconces are a great, inexpensive way to add light without a table.

WARM WELCOMES AND SUPPORTIVE SEND-OFFS

Welcome yourself into your own home! Wall art you love does this well, but many things can do the job of connecting you to your home as soon as you walk in. What works best is to feature something you think is beautiful, something personal, or (ideally) both. The welcoming element can be an inspiring quote painted on the wall, a smiling statue, or something else that says, "Welcome home, [insert your name]." Think about quotes, words, symbols, and other things that you will want to see when you walk in the door and things that make you feel connected and supported as you leave. In our entryway, I have a rotating set of wooden letters that form words I want to express to myself and my family. Sometimes I assemble the letters to say PRAY, and sometimes I put them together to say BREATHE. They've also said SLOW DOWN and HEE HEE. These are the things I want to see when I come home and especially when I'm going out. Some people prefer pictures, Bible verses, or plants. Do what works for you.

The welcome "sign" may have to live on an opposing wall or be somewhat separate from where you deposit all your stuff, but make sure to put your welcome in a place you'll see as soon as you walk in. Lots of people use mirrors opposite their front door. Although this has functional value, it is a bit impersonal, and it can be jarring to see yourself as you walk in carrying bags, children, or both, perhaps tired and weary. I am a fan of mirrors in bathrooms or opposite windows in dark rooms. For the entryway, put up something that makes you feel good and reminds you of something extraordinary in your life. If you have the room, create a space underneath the art on the walls for other things you enjoy looking at, such as meaningful books or collections. People often reserve their favorite things for huge, clunky armoires or étagères stuck in a corner somewhere. I am a fan of putting the things I love everywhere, spread out, and especially in places I look at often, as in the entryway.

Like so many high-use areas of the house, the entryway can make or break you. It seems inconsequential, especially when you can throw your mail or coat on a chair so easily. But this doesn't last, and systems that accommodate all the stuff you bring in and take out do make a difference in your quality of life and the order of your house. Furthermore, if you think through giving yourself visual pleasure when you walk in, you'll be rewarded, especially on those crummy days when the world has been unkind to you. Make your house work for you, especially when you need it.

YOUR TURN
WELCOME YOURSELF BETTER

Give yourself an hour this weekend and pretend you're a visitor to your own house. Walk in and out a few times, making mental notes about how it's all working. How do you feel when you walk in? What's the first thing you see?

IF IT'S DISORGANIZED

What could be more organized or put away more neatly? Outerwear? Bags? Books? Shoes? Choose the things that are always out and unsightly (to you) and find beautiful containers to house them—one each for you and everyone else in the house. If you live alone, have one for yourself and one for guests, presuming the "things" are shoes, coats, or bags. If you love your keys, find the brightest, most interesting, most intriguing bowl you can in a place that sells pottery. Putting keys into something pretty is an easier habit to keep up.

IF IT'S DEPRESSING

What is the first surface you see when you walk in? What is the first thing you notice? How can you address that space? If it's a wall, hang something you want to look at on it. Don't run out and buy something; start with something you already have and really like, and put it in this prominent place, even if it's a great photo of someone you love, stuck up with a thumbtack. If there's a tabletop or surface of some sort, can you put something you love on this surface? If you have pets or children and you can't put anything you really care about here, can you put up a hard-to-reach shelf nearby that can be just as visible as you walk in the door? The idea here is not to go and buy something for the entryway but to insert something right away that you already love and use it there for now. Perk up the energy before you buy anything new.

AS YOU LEAVE THE HOUSE

What's the last thing you see as you leave? Whether it's the back of the front door or a tiny corner next to the door, put something little that you love there—a wink to send you off into the world.

25

WHAT'S YOUR KITCHEN PERSONALITY?

*Establish your cooking, eating,
and entertaining aesthetic.*

Let's say for now the fundamental elements of your kitchen—layout, countertop, cabinets, appliances—are not going to change. How could it be more you without changing these things? The backdrop may be boring, but the personality of the space really comes from how we cook, how we eat, and what we want to surround ourselves with while we do these things. The color and texture of the walls, the tools and spices of the chef, the elements of everyday life, as well as decorative accessories, compose the look and feel of your kitchen more than larger features like cabinets.

You, not the perfect spread in *House Beautiful*, must be the constant reference point for what's right for your kitchen. Can you make it reflect what you like to cook and eat? What about your life story applies to the kitchen? Now is the time to think back to the kitchens and meals of childhood or travel that stuck with you. It's also time to consider your daily routine and what you use every day. If stuff is out all the time, is it stuff you enjoy looking at? If not, can you put it away or somehow make it more beautiful? Even appliances, like coffee makers, can be prettier tucked into a pretty tray or alongside an interesting sugar bowl or against a textured backdrop.

When traveling to homes in Europe and South America, I notice much more kitchenware hung up on walls—from copper pots to giant whisks and dozens of pot lids. Cooks in other countries tend to keep their tools out more often than we do here. We tuck almost everything away. If you love to cook or bake, or you do neither but like the look of your tools, why not keep them out on shelves/counters or wall hooks? I prefer to hang things on the wall rather than having them live on the counter. I've used baskets hung on walls to hold utensils and plate racks to organize pot lids. See if this works for you to keep your favorites visible.

Mix things up and use what you like. If you love color, there is no reason not to use it in the kitchen. Think about all the surfaces that can take paint (all of them). Don't feel compelled to match things perfectly. I have three different kinds of cabinets: some are covered in chalkboard paint, some are wood, and some are white. It all works because this matches my kitchen personality—colorful, expressive, and busy. If you like texture, there is no reason not to use that in your kitchen either. Perhaps you can apply a textured wallpaper, made for wet spaces, to the cabinet doors. Pay attention to the feel of all the hardware or kitchen tools you buy; you're going to handle it every day.

Changing cabinet hardware, lighting, window treatments, and even the faucet can be done without spending a lot of money. These changes, along with paint, go a long way. Longer than many people realize. Aesthetics are about details and big shapes in balance. How can you diminish the impact of those big elements you can't change right now? Can you paint the cabinets? Use an area rug? Downplay the countertops somehow by showing less of them? Beautiful decorative trays that hold often-used appliances, a gorgeous fruit bowl, even an oversized butcher-block-style cutting board can hide a lot of surface that you don't like. Here are the top three surface changes for the kitchen.

PAINTING CABINETS

Painting cabinets is a ton of work, but it's absolutely worth it. Painting your cabinets an interesting color that suits your kitchen personality is a game changer. You can successfully change the color of cabinets even if they are laminate and not wood. You need to know your DIY aptitude and exactly what the project entails before you start.

> *Eating is so intimate. It's very sensual. When you invite someone to sit at your table and you want to cook for them, you're inviting a person into your life.*
>
> **—MAYA ANGELOU**

Cabinets gather a lovely grease and dust sludge (at least in my house), so you should clean them well with degreasing solvents that will also rough up the surface a bit to prep them for painting. Remove all the doors and hardware, keeping everything well organized; I suggest lots of labeled plastic bags. Every surface to be painted needs a modest sanding. Your goal is not to remove the existing finish or paint; you just need to scratch up the surface to help the new paint adhere.

Once the cabinets are cleaned and sanded, they must be primed with a good-quality primer. (Don't use primer-and-top-coat-in-one for this project.) Give the primer coat a light sand, then end with two coats of semigloss paint.

When choosing a cabinet paint color, the world is your oyster. You're doing all the work, so do you want emerald green cabinets? Go for it! Often clients want white cabinets when they have dark cabinetry. Think beyond white, or more to the point, think of all the options within this color—the nuanced whites that have a hint of cream, pink, yellow, sand, or even gray to them. This is a bit more interesting than plain white cabinets and also serves to lighten up the space.

MAXIMIZING LIGHTING

We need light to perform all our kitchen tasks, and light is also interpreted as cleanliness, something we all desire in a space where we deal with food. First, take a hard look at the big three again: counters, cabinets, and flooring. Which is sucking the light out of your kitchen? Nonreflective (matte) surfaces in darker hues somehow extract light out of a space. If this describes what you have, find a way to change it inexpensively. A bright area rug in a lighter hue can really liven up a dark floor.

Focus on lighting sources next. You need a well-lit space in which to prepare food and see what you're doing. If all you have

Furniture and the Case of Kitchen Cabinets That Don't Match

Yes, you can use other kinds of furniture—like armoires, trunks, bookshelves, and desks— in your kitchen. Bring in whatever works for your needs; frankly, less cabinetry makes for a more interesting space. You can also mix two or even three styles of cabinetry. Or create a new work center with some kind of contrasting cabinet style.

is a centered ceiling fixture, see how you can up the ante on the available light by bringing in a fixture with multiple bulbs in higher wattages. If you don't have any other fixed lighting options, consider under-cabinet lighting, which can be either battery-powered or plug-in and is relatively inexpensive. IKEA has great options for this. What about wall sconces that plug in? They're used most often in the bedroom, above bedside tables, but why not in the kitchen? It's a little trickier to hide the cords in the kitchen, but you can buy tracks or channels to cover the cords and paint the tracks to match your walls. You probably can't "overlight" your kitchen; it's a space that benefits from as much light as possible, especially if you have darker surfaces to contend with.

How about bigger windows? If you are resigned to keeping everything as it is and not replacing the floor, cabinets, and countertops, you may elect to put your money into a bigger window. Making changes to the envelope, meaning the exterior of your house, is expensive and not within a small-kitchen-remake budget. It will likely cost you from $500 to $1,000 or more, depending on how big you want the window to be. However, bringing more light—and with it more of a pretty view and more fresh air—into a dark kitchen may be just the ticket to make your kitchen more enjoyable.

How can you better use the windows you do have? Refrain from hanging any window treatments that cover even a tiny fraction of the window. Something decorative (meaning it has no light-filtering or privacy function) like a valance or cornice *above* the window will frame and add color without stopping any light from coming in. If you prefer some level of privacy, consider translucent options such as solar shades, sheers, operable blinds, or shutters that can open clear of the window.

USE YOUR WALLS

Infuse personality into your kitchen with art. Framed photography, prints, beautiful plates—whatever you like to look at will work. Series, such as my family's three photos from cheese markets, work well in kitchens.

When considering surface treatment changes—those elements that really bring your personality into the space—you're doing this for you. You're doing it in a way that won't be all that hard for the next occupant of your house to change, so there isn't much risk. And it's likely that potential buyers will appreciate the personal touches you use to liven up what can be a bland, soulless space. Take chances, try a variety of colors and finishes, and don't copy other people's work. Keep your eyes on your own story.

What about a Kitchen Renovation?

There are three ways to get a new kitchen. The first option is to do a complete overhaul, removing everything currently in the kitchen and possibly taking out walls to enlarge or change the shape of the overall space. This option allows you to put new things—sink, appliances, and cabinets—back in entirely different locations. If your flow is awkward, or you're hoping for more counter space or a more open look, this is what you may want to do. An overhaul involves nearly every construction trade, takes the longest, and is the most expensive project to do in any house. The materials are expensive; there are structural, plumbing, and electrical implications of moving stuff around; and few people can do it without going over $50,000.

The second option is to retain the original kitchen layout and the location of the appliances, cabinets, windows, and doors, and simply replace everything. If your space works for you, but you hate the color of the cabinets or the appliances are old, this option may be appealing and is a lot less expensive than an overhaul. Of course, if you're replacing a lot of cabinets and buying new appliances, you may still spend $25,000.

A third renovation option involves one big change to the shape of the space or moving the locations of the major elements, but you don't replace everything. This is a good option if you like the cabinets and don't need to replace appliances, but the space could be more open or shifted in some way for better flow.

Whether you choose a complete overhaul, a replacement job, or a hybrid of some sort, consider what the problems are with what you currently have. Think about how you live as a cook, an eater, and a host, then think about whether classic kitchen components work for you or if you want to do something unique.

It's time to review how you live in your kitchen. Change your focus from all of your kitchen's shortcomings and take some time to think hard about the kind of cook, host, and eater you are. Think about daily routines and special occasions. Consider that small tweaks can accommodate your personality even better than sweeping changes, putting personal details that make life easier and more enjoyable right in front of you. From the answers below, find five small changes you can make to bring your personality into the room, this weekend. This may be as simple as finding an interesting ceramic planter to hold your often-used kitchen tools on the countertop. It may be repainting walls, but it can also be finding your color in a new tea pot. It could be a new backsplash, but it can also be hanging plates, putting away ugly appliances, or finding just the right tray to corral them.

1   *How do you start your day? Is this set up properly for you?*

2   *What tools do you use every day? Is there a beautiful way to arrange them?*

3   *What colors inspire you as you cook? As an eater? Can you use both more in your kitchen?*

4   What are some decorative items from another part of the house that you love that could work in the kitchen?

5   How do you want your kitchen to feel?

Consider the following options for personalization, and choose one of them as a project for the soonest available weekend. The whole list gets overwhelming, even though they are all technically small fixes.

- Swapping out or mixing up cabinet hardware, changing cabinet paint color, removing cabinet doors
- Changing overhead lighting, adding wall lighting
- Adding backsplash texture, mixing in interesting and colorful countertop accessories and appliances
- Putting up wall-mounted shelves, bins, or storage such as a pot or lid rack
- Replacing the kitchen faucet
- Painting the walls or ceiling a new color, adding textures like cork or chalkboard to walls or cabinet faces

These are changes that make a kitchen personal—what two can you focus on to start?

Bathrooms are, on a square-foot basis, the most expensive room in the house to renovate. If you want to test your heart's fitness, try shopping for simple bathroom faucets. Add in the cost of the required valves, mixers, and trims, and you may need reviving when you see the tally!

—CANDICE OLSON

26

MAKING PEACE WITH YOUR BATHROOM

*What do you do with a bathroom
that isn't going anywhere soon but
you still can't live with?*

The most common complaint about unloved bathrooms is the color of the tile, specifically bathrooms from the 1950s in Easter egg hues of pink, peach, and minty green. Then there are their condiment-colored counterparts from the sixties and seventies, resplendent in avocado green, mustard yellow, and hummus-like tan. Or you may have an awesome eighties bathroom, no doubt influenced by the aesthetics of Michael Jackson or Liberace, with black fixtures, red accents, and lots of brass and mirrors everywhere. If all you really want is a bathroom that doesn't scream a previous decade, but you can't afford to gut the whole thing, take heart. There are things you can do to mute even the worst trends of yesteryear.

You have the same three options here that I discussed in the kitchen chapter. You can remove and replace everything in the bathroom from toilet paper holder to tile, possibly moving things around and enlarging the space in some way while you're at it. You can simply paint or recover things that are old, in disrepair, or ugly—walls, flooring, tile—and replace the fixtures that are easy and less expensive such as the faucet, towel bars, and lighting. Or you can do the hybrid approach of changing some parts and leaving others. Please do your homework before launching into a blitz of quick fixes. Consult the Internet for techniques, but go with your heart for ideas on color, mood, and what will delight you when you use this room. If you do decide to pursue a larger renovation, the National Kitchen & Bath Association (NKBA) offers a long list of ideal design guidelines, some of which mirror local building codes. They are worth looking at if you're wondering how you might rework the shape of your bathroom and location of your fixtures (www.nkba.org). Here are some approaches when a large scale renovation isn't possible but big change is needed.

JUST GO WITH IT

This doesn't work for everyone or every bathroom, but sometimes going with what you've got, rather than fighting it, is the thing to do. It also helps if you appreciate your home's vintage. If you live in a house born of the 1950s, you have a lot of legitimate midcentury modern design around you. Even if you'd much rather live in a Victorian, you don't, so why not work with what you have? If you look, you are likely to find aspects of midcentury design that appeal to you.

Perhaps you are the proud owner of a "pink lady" bathroom from the fifties. Like a satin jacket from a community theater production of *Grease*, it may offend you and fail to follow the neutrals and subdued palette you prefer. There are ways, however, to turn all that kitsch into something that appeals to you. Art deco, pink, and black was a threesome made in heaven. Can you find art deco-inspired lighting that you like? The details of deco command attention, so there is likely to be less focus on all that pink. How about framed fashion sketches from the 1950s, which are likely to have their fair share of black and pink? What about an expressive black-and-white wallpaper, to fight fire with fire? Metal, specifically chrome, harmonizes all that color exceptionally well. Consider what period fixtures and accessories you can add that take some of the attention away from the color you dislike, if it's not deco. *Rejuvenation* is an exceptional catalog for good-quality, American-made period lighting fixtures, including positively dashing chrome fixtures that will take center stage. If you ride the tide of what you've been given, it will still be 80 percent pink and black, but that new 20 percent can comprise all the details such as artwork, metals, and accessories that make you happy and make it yours.

DETAILS

Bathrooms and kitchens are all about the details; details set the tone for the kind of bathroom you want to create. The cabinet hardware, lighting, area rugs, hand towels, framed art, and small shelf with pretty things to look at are more meaningful than the larger changes you may not be able to afford right now. I'm not just telling you that to make you feel better. Even if you were to make the sweeping changes, it's the small details that make a room yours. Make your selections carefully, and don't limit yourself to the options at the big-box retailers or whatever is available at your local lighting store. The Internet has made resources for details an embarrassment of riches. It can be overwhelming, which is why it's important to be clear on your aesthetic first, lest you find yourself paging through two thousand wall sconces.

HEAVY METAL

Metal choices are key components in a bathroom. If you hate all the brass, there are other choices you can use to replace it on everything from cabinet hardware and plumbing fixtures to towel bars and lighting. Don't consider only brushed nickel; there are multiple forms of bronze, black iron, white porcelain, and chrome available as well. Wait until you see what just switching out the metal does for a dated bathroom. That and painting the walls your perfect color can take you more than halfway to bathroom love.

If it suits your vision, explore some vintage looks and see what appeals to you. If you make a commitment to historic restoration, that's great, but don't feel committed to historical accuracy. This is your house. If your bathroom is from the 1950s but there are features from the 1920s that speak to you and work in the space, go with what you like. The idea is to fall in love with the details and let the background recede a bit.

PAINT

In smaller spaces, the paint color choice is important. In bathrooms that typically have more artificial lighting than natural light, walls that face each other, and semigloss paint, color is all the more critical. I'm a fan of warm whites for warm tile colors (with hints of peach, pink, orange) and bright whites for cool colors (blue with just a touch of gray or minty green). Warm white softens the pink a lot, and bright white seems to brighten even the drabbest greens and blues.

TILE

If you do decide to buy new tile, the bigger the tile, the lower the cost of your project. When you use a larger tile, such as 12 × 12-inch squares, you need fewer of them and, by extension, less grout. Fewer tiles need to be cut with a specialized wet saw, and they are easier to work with than any smaller tile—even those with a mesh backing. If you are using tile for the first time, pick something big.

If you are trying to save money, pick something big. Big has other benefits too. Bigger tiles can make a small bathroom feel bigger with fewer grout lines to clean. Remember that you don't always have to arrange tiles in a perfect grid; you can position them in a brick format (also known as subway tile pattern) or on the diagonal, which is more interesting.

Painting tile is an imperfect option but worth pursuing if you have the elbow grease and no money to replace the tile. If you simply cannot live with the tile color, it's worth going after what you like, whether it's replacing what's there (perhaps in a smaller footprint to save money, such as on the floor but not on the walls); painting it; or covering the wall tile with beadboard paneling made from PVC.

TUB AND SHOWER

Tub refinishing is not a new idea and can cost between $300 and $600, depending on where you live. It involves a smelly sprayed application of an epoxy paint product. The finish will look great and can last, but it will be much more delicate than the original tub you have from the seventies. Any tubs constructed of cast iron, porcelain, or fiberglass can be refinished. Replacing the big fixtures (tub, sink, and toilet) with white ones and leaving the wall and floor tile as-is is an interesting option. There was a time when it was cool to have everything match—peach tub, peach sink, peach toilet, peach floor. It's probably less expensive to simply switch out the toilet (about $300 installed), replace the sink/vanity (about $300 to $1,000 installed), and refinish the tub (about $450) than it is to replace the tile. Plus, new white fixtures that work well against whatever tile you have will give you a completely different bathroom. The tile, if it's in decent condition, may have a lovely vintage quality that you'll appreciate more if you can sit on a new toilet, have the convenience of a new sink, or can bathe in a white tub.

TOILET

There is a great variance in toilet quality and price, and the more people using the toilet, the more it pays to choose a better-quality one. You could also modify this equation: the more teenage boys and men who use the bathroom, the better off you'll be buying a higher-end toilet. I'm very fond of the Toto brand models in our house. They rarely, if ever, clog. They are supposed to never clog, but nothing is that good. Four males use our Totos daily, which is my anecdotal testament to the brand. Every plumber has a favorite. My plumber, Jimmy, who has three sons, uses Totos exclusively.

LAVATORY (SINK)

Sinks cannot be refinished like tubs, but a simple pedestal sink in white will cost a few hundred dollars installed. Not only is a pedestal affordable, it also opens up a small bathroom by clearing out the floor space. It does mean absolutely no storage under the sink, which some bathrooms sorely need. If you really want a new sink, go for a decent-quality pedestal, and make up the storage with wall cabinets and shelving rather than a vanity with an underneath cabinet that is just so-so.

If you have a cheap vanity or something that doesn't suit you, what shape is it in? Find out what it's made of. Take a look behind and inside the doors and drawers, if applicable. If there isn't any water damage or splitting and it's relatively solid, painting it as you would a piece of furniture is a great way to give it new life. Do not paint something that's damaged or broken. If you strongly prefer a vanity, don't get the biggest one that will fit in your space. It may be tempting to buy something that will just fit and afford you lots of storage, but this will backfire. A bathroom with no breathing room will frustrate you more than the color schemes and dated details that got you working on this room in the first place.

Often the sink is the visual marker for the room—the hardware, the bowl itself, and the vanity or pedestal are usually the first things you see. If you have to pick one large fixture to change out, make it the sink. You also spend the most time facing it and looking right at it when you're in the bathroom; the other fixtures get less direct attention or can be obscured by shower curtains.

Bathrooms aren't the heart of the house, but they are the gut; you don't look at them all the time, but if they don't work, it hurts. Focus on what you want and what you've liked in other bathrooms you've used (as opposed to those you've just seen online or in magazines). Don't discount any element or detail as something that "doesn't matter." It all matters. You might say, "It's only a towel bar," which I suppose is true. But it's a towel bar you'll likely use every day. It can be boring and hardly noticeable, or it can be interesting and add something like a positive thought to your day, every day for years! Making sure it's what you really want is worth it.

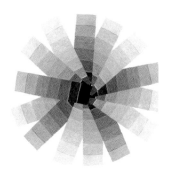

YOUR TURN

GO WITH IT OR GO IN
ANOTHER DIRECTION?

It's time to decide whether you are going to take the baton your
bathroom offers, work with the vintage or existing look, and build on
it or whether you are going to go in an entirely different direction.

1   List your five major complaints about this bathroom in your
    Home Book.

2   Next, make a list of all the little things (anything aside from the
    tub, sink, toilet, or tile) that can easily come out with either your
    elbow grease or the help of a handyman.

3   Before any shopping takes place, write down what your
    bathroom aesthetic is in words. How do you meld what you
    have in the rest of your house, as well as your life's story, into a
    bathroom space? What colors that you love will you introduce
    into this space? What shapes are you drawn to when it comes
    time to pick new lighting, hardware, and so on?

4   With your list of possible replaceable items and your aesthetic
    words to shop by, pick one project per weekend for a month.
    This pace allows each new choice to build on the previous one.

168 LOVE THE HOUSE YOU'RE IN

27

WHAT HAPPENS IN YOUR BEDROOM?

This is the easiest room in the house
in which to make high-impact change—
and the most intimate.

The bedroom is the last space most people work on. Married
people, especially, assume no one outside the family will ever
see the bedroom, and they figure they can simply close the door
to shut their childhood bureau, bare walls, piles of laundry, or
overdue/unread library books away from the world.

Don't put your bedroom last on your list. We hopefully get
seven or eight hours of sleep a night. Let's say we spend a total
of one hour a day getting dressed or undressed and stocking our
bedroom with clean laundry. Not only are we spending eight to ten
hours a day in this room, we are entering it when we are tired and
in great need of rest. We need a space that relaxes us and makes
us feel both welcome and comforted. We need to feel at home
here as much as in our living rooms or kitchens.

The key to a great bedroom is making it as sensually personal
as possible. I'm not talking about sex (yet). I'm talking about making
it appealing to all your senses. Make sure this is a personal and
intimate space that fits you like a glove, not only in terms of what
you see but in what you touch, hear, and smell, too.

My bedroom is a very important space in my home. Our house is relatively small, and our family is relatively large. Consequently, parent-only time barely exists; when it does, it is in our bedroom. I wanted it to be a distinctly adult space with more subdued colors to offset our Technicolor life with our kids and their things. It was also important to me to balance feminine and masculine in the space. Inspired by the whites and blues of our seaside adventures together, as well as some great hotels we've stayed in over the years, I used my all-time favorite neutral—Benjamin Moore's Manchester Tan HC-81 (which is neither tan nor particularly English)—on the walls. I originally preferred a dark blue color on the walls, but our bedroom is small, with low ceilings and walls that aren't straight. I know that lying in bed looking at a crooked or imperfect blue line where dark blue paint met the ceiling along the not-perfectly plumb walls would be some kind of punishment for my husband. The tan paint was just enough color and more forgiving than a dark wall color would have been. I used navy and salmon sparingly, with lots of different shades of white and cream. I have an old, thin, tarnished-brass crucifix over my bed, and pictures of our prechild adventures in a gallery on one wall. Other than that, the room is quiet and simply put together. I love it. The result is a space in which my husband and I can connect and be refreshed for the next day. It feels both Spartan and adult.

Let's consider what you're trying to accomplish in a bedroom. For every element in the room, keep in mind that couples often struggle with balancing what both parties find beautiful, interesting, or comfortable. There is a lot of give-and-take, but I find that if the space represents both halves of a couple, it is more likely a place where both will feel rested and cherished, even if only one party puts the room together. (Which is how it is in our house.) It takes negotiation, listening, and consideration of two sets of preferences when it comes to colors, textures, and what is sensually pleasing.

PREPARING FOR SLEEP

What do you need to relax? Do you like soft music? Do you need low lighting? Some of these things are universal. If you ask sleep specialists, they'll likely recommend the following for a good night's rest: as few bright computer screens as possible, no overhead lighting, the same bedtime each night, and the smell of lavender. The rest is really up to you. What do you need by your bedside? Books? A candle that smells good? A device that plays music? Nothing? If you don't need a vase and a picture of your parents and a dog-training book, then perhaps these things don't need to live on your bedside table.

Preparing for sleep also means having your day clothing easy to put away and your night clothing easy to find. It means making sure you are the right temperature. Notice I haven't said anything about a modern platform bed versus a traditional four-poster. And not because I hate the words *modern* and *traditional* in this context, although I do. I want you to think about what you need for all your senses to prepare for bed as essential parts of putting your bedroom together.

Think about the colors you find soothing. Are they reminiscent of the beach? Are they the colors of the night sky? Are they the jewel tones of your native India? Whatever they are, choose your bedroom wall color carefully. When you have an idea of what kinds of colors you might like, test the color on the wall with a small amount of paint on a patch near your bed so you can see it at nighttime, with artificial light, and during the day, ideally with morning light if you get any in your bedroom. I always recommend picking an extreme in the bedroom. There is something soothing about very dark colors in this room—navy, slate, even a dark burgundy—and something calming about much lighter-hued paints with just a whisper of color. Be sure to test whatever you choose at both times you'll be in bed, night and day.

SLEEP

To get a good night's rest, you need a good bed. A good bed is not only a frame, headboard, and/or footboard, it is also a good mattress. It is good sheets, blankets, coverlets, and pillows—a layer cake of goodness. If you can't afford a new bed frame or mattress, consider it an important renovation project to upgrade everything on your bed: invest in a good-quality mattress cover (the thicker ones can mimic a more expensive mattress), and build a collection of fabulous linens for all the beds in the house.

My dear childhood friend Christina Bozarth is an unabashed linens guru. She always has the most sumptuous bedding—starchy white but soft, fresh, and abundant—throughout her house. I hate to get out of bed when I'm visiting her. Christina doesn't just make a bed; she dresses it (her words) just as she dresses herself, with attention to details and comfort but great simplicity in the end result. She includes dashes of color and texture here and there with pillows and pillowcases. She also uses layers on layers, even in summer, to allow for the sleeper to choose what he or she needs based on temperature and comfort. She has taught me that bedding that feels good ends up looking good to boot.

Even if you have to skimp somewhere else, even if your bed is old and uncomfortable, even if you think it doesn't matter, buy good sheets for all the beds in your house. Not necessarily expensive but sheets that feel good to you. This makes making those beds easier, and it also means *all* the beds will feel good to sleep in. (This is especially helpful when your children ask you to lie down in their beds.) Another tip is to buy most of your bedding in white or cream; that way the sheets are interchangeable to make a complete set when you make the bed. You need not buy whole sets, just individual sheets when and

> *My apartment is my stage, and my bedroom is my stage—they're just not stages you're allowed to see.*
>
> **—LADY GAGA**

where you care to. You can customize the beds with colorful pillows, pillowcases, and coverlets. I like my bed made of white sheets with all different textures and white-on-white patterns. A wardrobe of great, interchangeable linens happens over time. Next time you're on a trip and are looking for something to bring home, why not look at bed linens? This is a different twist on connecting your travels to your house in a delightfully useful way. Become acquainted with all the words to describe sheets to find the ones that feel best to you; touch, feel, and experiment with pima cotton, sateen, linen, and other natural fibers.

CONNECTING WITH YOUR PARTNER AND HAVING SEX

I am not a sex therapist, and this is still a design book. However, your environment matters, and paying attention to each space means you're paying attention to what you'd like to have happen in that space. So paying attention to your bedroom and ensuring that it is comfortable and accommodating and captures the soul of each half of a couple, means also paying attention to your sex life. You are creating an environment that allows for good things to happen. If you enjoy cooking with lots of different herbs and spices, you wouldn't forget to make space for them in your kitchen, right? If you enjoy having a good sex life with your partner or spouse, make sure your bedroom has what it needs to make this happen.

One could argue that intimacy happens when both people have enough time, inclination, and privacy (certainly invest in a lock on your bedroom door if you have children). I think it goes further. Think about the things that are important to your intimate life: Music? Lighting? Media? (No judgment here!) The bottom line is that thoughtfulness will go a long way. Consider what senses—visual, aural, and olfactory—you want to enhance for whatever you want to happen in your bedroom.

KEEP CLOTHING ORGANIZED

What works best for you to keep your clothes off the floor and the bed, and in the closets or dresser drawers? Feel free to break out of the traditional bedroom furniture model (bed, night table, bureau); it doesn't work for everyone. It's key to have a place for clothing for all seasons, clean and dirty, as well as accessories. I prefer not to look at any of this, so I like floor-to-ceiling armoires. I can close the door on the often-unkempt state of my closet. It helps me sleep better. I have worked with families that made their bedrooms much smaller to incorporate a walk-in closet so their bedroom could be just that: a room for the bed. I've also worked with people who held dear their traditional bedroom furniture that had been passed down for generations—for these people, the dresser became a showpiece *and* a repository for clothes. What do you want to look at from your bed? How do you want to store your clothing?

GETTING DRESSED

If you have a walk-in closet and are able to keep your clothing out of your bedroom, I'm jealous; you're able to keep your bedroom much simpler and clutter-free. Try to keep all of your stuff in that closet and resist the temptation to keep a dresser and some storage in the room itself. If you need a surface for jewelry or things you like to keep out and look at, consider a wall-mounted shelf that you can hang at any height you like. These shelves also come in spans as wide as six feet, offering much more ample space than a standard dresser can. When you furnish your bedroom, take into account door swings and drawer-pull-out ranges when you choose your pieces so it doesn't get overfurnished and too tight.

A key to a peaceful bedroom is for everyone to have enough room to move around. This is a luxury we don't all have, but we can make the most of a small space by using our full ceiling height and making sure everything fits in the room before buying it. Bring along a good 2-D floor plan of your bedroom when you're furniture shopping.

If you are shopping for your bedroom, most retailers are happy to show you their bedside tables, their bureaus or dressers, and their bed frames. Don't limit yourself to the bedroom department for your bedroom furniture. Some small desks and small cabinets meant for offices or media rooms or kitchens work very well as bedside tables. Consider your space and what you need to organize, and go from there.

RELAX AND BE ENTERTAINED

Whether to have a television in their bedroom is a conundrum some couples face, while others wouldn't last one night without a 50-inch TV two feet from their faces. I have no opinion on whether it's good for marriage or not. I do feel that if both partners are interested in watching television together, then this is an experience that should be honored in the bedroom. Small spaces present challenges, and often it's the TV, not the clothes, that warrant the purchase of a large dresser or bureau. As a matter of full disclosure, I love watching TV but hate actually looking at TVs when they are not on. Yes, they've gotten more streamlined and sleek in the last ten years, but they are still not what I want to look at unless I'm watching something on them.

There are all sorts of solutions for hiding TVs, most of which are most easily accomplished if you simply have a bigger bedroom. Don't hide the TV, but try not to allow it to dominate your space. Keep it lower on the wall—eye-level when you're in bed is lower than you realize. Also, you may consider painting the wall behind the TV a dark color, muting the contrast between a black plastic TV structure and a light-colored wall. Or draw your attention elsewhere by placing prominent art you enjoy on other walls. You can also frame out the TV with smaller framed pictures and art to blunt the impact of the TV on its wall. Don't fight it. Black frames clustered in rectangular series on opposing walls complement and balance the TV rather than letting it stick out like a sore thumb.

PREPARE FOR THE DAY

Your bedroom is not only your sanctuary at night, it is also the space that prepares you for the rest of your day. Take time to think about what you need to start your day well: Do you want a breath of fresh air? A moment in prayer? Time to review your calendar? A mirror? Easy access to your robe or slippers? Music? News? Think critically about what you need, and make sure that what you have in your bedroom accommodates this.

It's easy to phone in the bedroom because "it's just us" that sees it. You do a lot more than just sleep there, and the bedroom is where your day begins. If you start out by hitting your shin on a dresser that sticks out too much, not being able to find your socks, or realizing that your wife's favorite art looks downright demonic in the light of dawn, perhaps some changes to your storage and wall hangings can improve the situation. We're not talking about the scale or complexity of change needed in the rest of the house—this is easy stuff, so don't put it at the end of your project list.

If you shift your thinking from saying, "I just sleep there," to considering yourself the most important consumer or audience, then you'll be more likely to give yourself a great bedroom with things that make you feel good, rested, rejuvenated, and ready for anything.

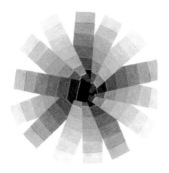

When you go to bed tonight, set aside an extra thirty minutes to hang out and take in your bedroom. How does it feel? What is there to look at? Are things out that you wish were away? Is the wall color pleasing? How does the bed feel? Is what you need for restful sleep handy and where it needs to be for your comfort? Ask your partner these questions too. What is the one thing, from the point of view of being in bed, that seems the most awful? Can you start working on it right away? If you are a morning person, this exercise can also be done right after you wake up.

28

ROOMS WITH CHILDREN

Living with children does not have to mean stained, broken, and worse, but it often does; it might as well be beautiful, interesting, and personal.

Kid chaos has many chapters. First, there is the tyrannical baby blob of oversized gear with Times Square-inspired lights and music. Then there is the beglittered preschool artwork and Legos, and before you know it, you're contending with sports equipment, musical instruments, ice skates, and more strewn about the house, beside the front door, and in the family car. If you are someone who likes order and organization or has an aversion to garish color schemes, you will need some sort of prescription medication until your children beat these qualities out of you.

There is a tendency for parents to say, "Our kids are little," or "Our kids make us so busy, we can't have anything nice." What the latter part of this statement means is different for everyone. If *nice* means expensive, easily marred, or altogether irreplaceable, you're probably right. But if it means something pleasing, interesting, or enjoyable for the adults, you're wrong. Parents need to make accommodations to their aesthetic when they have children—any number of children at any age. However, accommodation doesn't mean wholesale surrender. It doesn't mean a rewrite of what you would ideally want your house to look like and how you want it to work. Accommodations are strategic choices you make while your children are young and the gross years are in full swing, and later on, when school tuition or new soccer cleats for four render that fifty-dollar-a-yard fabric an impossibility.

But don't change what has always been important to you aesthetically even though children become a part of your home and budget. Your kids will add to your story, but they need not erase what was there before. Earlier in the book, you considered your early adult life, perhaps your prechild life—don't leave this out. If you have an all-white house with lots of breakables, there are certainly slightly less breakable, less stainable choices that can be made, but don't abandon the white or the glass altogether. Kids can live in a space and not wreck it, and learning how to do this, if imperfectly, is an important life skill. Your house won't always and may never be magazine-perfect, but the foundation can still be there—a backdrop to the noise and chaos that allows you and your spouse/partner to express yourselves and feel connected.

Most children threaten at times to run away from home. This is the only thing that keeps some parents going.

—PHYLLIS DILLER

The key to feeling like it's still your house and not a day-care center is to surround yourself with what you like. This may mean buying something new, refurbishing what you've been given, or holding on for dear life to what you had before your children came, even if it has a low chance of survival during the growing years. Here are some other things to keep in mind.

FABRICS THAT COME TO PLAY

There are miracle fabrics and treatments for upholstery in the stain battle royale, and the universe of "performance fabrics" has never been bigger. I'll never forget working on a project at Thomasville Furniture, when the woman I was speaking with (about these fabrics) beamed at me and said, "Parents don't have to choose dark fabrics anymore. There are hundreds of light-colored fabrics in our performance fabrics book." This is the good news. You don't have to choose brown microsuede unless you like brown microsuede. Another option is machine-washable or bleachable slipcovers, particularly if (really only if) you like white. This is a bit more work and upkeep, but certainly an option for the family couch.

OUTDOOR-TOUGH MEANS CHILD-TOUGH

The single biggest shift in home design and renovation has been a focus on outdoor living. With more and more families creating outdoor living spaces, furniture, rugs, and even upholstery are now made to withstand the elements and other menaces like mildew and mold for use outdoors. This is a boon to families with young children. Indoor/outdoor rugs are genius for life with kids. Almost always in a flat-woven style, outdoor rugs come in a wide choice of colors and price points. They even have indoor/outdoor rugs to mimic sisal and other natural fiber rugs that are not stain-tolerant.

Friends are aghast to find that I have light-colored rugs in my house with three sons. They don't know that anytime I need to, I can hose them down in my backyard (the rugs, not the kids). I have yet to go that far, because any kind of mess my sons have produced, from drippy popsicles to sludge from shoes, has come clean with a wet rag and minimal soap. This is because indoor/outdoor rugs are typically woven polypropylene—a thermoplastic polymer used in a variety of industrial applications as well as outdoor-friendly woven textiles. Yes, it's plastic, but it does a great job of mimicking a naturally derived textile.

PUT IT OUT OF REACH

I can remember when my pediatrician told me to put away my breakables when my oldest son started walking as a prodigal nine-month-old. I thought to myself, *I'll never put away anything.* Naturally I had no idea what I was in for, and many broken pretties later, I've done my share of trial and error in the keep-it-out-but-safe area. One strategy that's been most successful for me is to use the height of my space. This is a nice way of saying, "Put nice stuff out, but where the kids can't reach it."

Plenty of parents can safely return their lovely breakables to tabletop surfaces once their children are four or five years old. I cannot. I live with boys who have an unstoppable need to run, wrestle, and see how easily things break. Keeping things at table-height doesn't work in my house, so I use high shelving.

Choose shelves that are beautiful on their own, with hardware and brackets that are either hidden from view or interesting to you, as you'll be looking at the underside of them a lot of the time. Put them above doorways, along the perimeter of a room, anywhere you can see what's on them but where they can't be reached by tiny hands. These shelves are my little treasure chests of things I don't need my children seeing (such as my copy of *Bitch in the House*); things I don't want them to break (lovely flea-market-found milk glass); and things I just enjoy more from afar (heirloom Hummel figurines from my late mother-in-law). High shelves can be purchased anywhere from IKEA to Horchow, and they come in a variety of textures and materials. They also add an architectural feature to spaces that are short on trim work or other interesting details.

FINGER PAINTING ON THE WALLS—WITH KETCHUP

There are tidiness tips to keep in mind for your home with children that don't alter your aesthetic but help you keep the smudgy kid messes, if not to a minimum, then to a level you can handle. Magic Eraser by Mr. Clean is a parent's best friend. You probably don't need a new paint job, you just need a Magic Eraser. It cleans almost anything (crayon, pencil, grease, blood, worse) off any hard surface, including matte walls. Unless you're scrubbing a white wall, you'll need to rinse the residue away. I wish they came by the case.

It's certainly worth using paint that can be scrubbed when you have children. Typically, semigloss paint is the easiest to clean and the most moisture-resistant. It's also typically reserved for bathrooms and kitchens, but why not the dining room where you feed your children? I've even worked with families who painted the bottom half of the wall—aka sticky-finger-height—in semigloss; added some kind of transition such as a chair rail, trim with hooks, plain trim, or a stripe of another color; and used flat-finish paint above it. Satin finish isn't quite as slippery and not as easy to clean as semigloss, but it's a good compromise if you prefer a matte wall but are also engaged in a dirty fingerprint battle.

Another paint strategy is to invite the kids to be more interactive than just plain messy. What if they were encouraged to write on the walls? You can use paint that is intended to be written on, such as chalkboard paint, IdeaPaint (great for teen rooms; see the next chapter), or magnetized paint, which can showcase all their lovely art *and* be written on. Why spend your time scrubbing when you can indulge your children in their self-expression and then simply wipe it or keep it as long as you wish?

BUYING "JUST FOR NOW"

Balance waiting and buying temporary things. Heed the need for self-expression amid the sea of cheaply made furniture, but limit your disposable furniture purchases. For instance, "This chair is so cute, and it's only $49!" And it won't last two years, most likely. Cheap furnishings certainly make sense on occasion, but allowing this kind of buying to dominate how you put your house together doesn't work; nothing lasts long enough to create a cohesive and lasting look and feel to your home. Each time you see something the kids will surely destroy that seems inexpensive enough for you not to care, you have to ask yourself, "Am I buying this because it's just going to get trashed by the kids anyway, or am I buying it because it's perfect for my entryway, and it's a cheap replica of something I love from my favorite hotel lobby?" The first case is disconnected buying. The second case is accommodation but committed, connected buying. Go for it—but not all the time.

CONSIDERING YOUR CHILD'S BEDROOM

Even spaces for children should be connected to the parents' aesthetic. No matter how in love your toddlers are with *The Wiggles*, your toddlers don't have an aesthetic of their own. It's your job to infuse their space with the playful parts of your story. When they are older, they will have different ideas and preferences, and you can work on the room together.

Ask yourself what you loved as a child and what you love now. Allow your child's room to reconnect you with your childhood.

CHILDREN WELCOME

I don't believe in white-glove rooms. There is no part of my house that my children aren't allowed to use. There is plenty they can't reach, but that's different. My house is hospitable to everyone—with rules. The kids know that on Mommy's couch, their hands have to be clean (often they're not). They know that crayons, markers, and pencils are for paper only (although I've found hieroglyphics on nearly every surface in my home). It's useful to have places that are primarily for children as well—places where they can jump on the furniture and revel in the thunder of a bin of toys being dumped onto the floor. But there are rules there too. The rules are never adhered to perfectly, and you will find stains and toy parts everywhere in my house, but I think a home full of interesting things hides stains and imperfections well.

Survival with kids means acceptance and patience. The survival of your *aesthetic* among kids means even more acceptance and more patience, as well as flexibility. I've learned to lower my expectations for the sake of my own sanity. It's my house, the way I want it, the way I love it. I'd rather have this version messed up from time to time—or all the time, depending on how busy or housebound we are—than a version I don't like with a set of placeholder furniture, which would be messed up just as often. I also want my children to live in my house and enjoy it, with proper limits. Learning that each room in the house is available to them *and* that each space has its own rules is a valuable lesson for kids, one they (or at least their future spouse) will appreciate later in life. They miss this lesson if everything in the house is considered too precious for them to use, or if there are no rules and nothing is "nice."

Evaluate New Purchases Before You Buy

Get the kid-hardiness education for everything before you buy. Ask furniture salespeople and friends who have similar products about anything new you're interested in getting, and read online reviews. Here are some good questions to ask: When this stains, what do I use to clean it? Can this be machine-washed? Can this be hosed down? Does this finish scratch easily? How do you remove marks made with a Sharpie? Do these chairs/benches/tables tip over easily? What happens if someone stands on top of them? Jumps on them? Bangs on them with a shoe?

Are you the parent who laments that your house is filled with stained and worn furniture and rugs, and you're biding your time until your kids are old enough to be less gross and grimy? If that is the case, consider a change to your space—an upgrade of some element in a communal space that would be hearty enough for the kids but beautiful enough to suit the aesthetic you've shelved while being a parent. Begin small, but slowly regain your space, aesthetically speaking.

1   *Name something gross and ugly in your space that you would love to replace.*

2   *Visualize what you'd like to have there if you weren't afraid the kids would ruin it.*

3   *Search out an option online like the one in your vision that is kid-hearty. Think outdoor rugs and fabrics or easy-care items.*

Or are you the parent who is terribly anxious about the couch, the rug, the breakables? Perhaps in that case, you might ease your anxiety and add some calm by replacing the rug or piece of furniture with one that has more stain-resistant qualities or is made for outdoor use. Loosen the grip—the kid and the furniture are more enjoyable when you aren't as worried.

1 *Name something in your house that you spend time worrying about, something you're afraid the kids will ruin.*

2 *Ask yourself if there is another location in your house, where the kids are less likely to be, for this item.*

3 *Consider a more stain-resistant or easy-care piece in its place, such as something with washable (and bleachable) slipcovers or accessories that are less expensive than heirlooms. The new choices may even look remarkably similar to the original(s). Or perhaps investing in high shelves will protect what you're concerned about while allowing you to look at it as you please.*

29

TEENAGE WASTELAND?

*Manage what your teen, like, totally
wants in his or her bedroom.*

As puberty represents the quantum leap between childhood and
adulthood, it is no wonder that teens start to want their own space
to truly reflect who they are or how they see themselves. They are
in fact developing their own aesthetic, like it or not. Given that
parents not only own everything but typically pay for everything
in their child's room and that the parents have lived twenty, thirty,
or even forty years longer than said child, it is no wonder that they
do not take kindly to a parcel of their property being swathed in
Taylor Swift or NFL posters, half-naked pictures of other teens,
and mile-high piles of clothes. So there's the conflict: a semiadult
wanting to express himself or herself versus true adults who
want this in principle but in practice have a tough time with it
happening inside their biggest asset.

Like everything else in your home, this is a creative process—
and a sacred one at that. Your teen's room will be a refuge from
the highs and lows of turbocharged hormones and Telenovela-
scale dramas, not to mention the packed schedules of kids who
partake in sixteen-hour days replete with school, sports, and music.
Home base for the average American teen is an important place
functionally as well as aesthetically.

Moms and dads, it *is* your house, but you'll do well to allow your teens to own their space in a manner you can live with. This can be a great collaborative project for a teen with one or both parents. It need not be expensive or elaborate. Teen design and decor has become a niche industry sparked by catalogs like PB Teen that showcase bikini-clad teens laughing and lounging amid surfboard desks and faux-fur lounge chairs. Who wouldn't want to live inside a PB Teen catalog? It all looks so fun. And while it may be better than a still from an episode of *Hoarders: Buried Alive* (which is what my teenage bedroom looked like at times), the spaces of PB Teen are extravagantly priced and out of reach for most parents.

Here is the good news: working on a room with your teen is a good time to teach him that it's boring and lame to copy a bunch of rooms created by nonteenagers to sell stuff, no matter how fabulous it looks in a magazine. It is, however, very cool to incorporate what makes him unique, what makes him happy, and what he needs for a room that helps him relax after a long day.

Take the creation of your teen's bedroom as seriously as you would your own bedroom, and establish the rules early. A good one to start with is, "We'll be working on this together, and you'll be heard." Another good one is, "I am going to be paying for some or all of this, and I get a vote too, maybe two." Your teen may be interested, if she is uninitiated in DIY projects, in learning about painting, furniture refinishing, window treatments, and possibly simple carpentry. Even if you don't know these skills yourself and are an avid outsourcer, your motivated teen, armed with YouTube tutorials and babysitting money, could get the furniture piece she wants desperately or build the loft bed he saw in a movie, and in doing so earn the boost of self-confidence and feeling of accomplishment that come from doing something by yourself. It's also a way for her to learn about DIY math, as in, "That PB Teen dresser costs $799, but this one on Craigslist costs $25. It needs a paint job, which costs $60 in materials and a weekend of your time."

PICKING FURNITURE

Let your teen lead the sourcing of the furniture for his room. Encourage him to look everywhere—yard sales, thrift stores, Craigslist, eBay, Etsy.com, Target, Walmart, and relatives' attics in addition to PB Teen, CB2, or other stores that may have caught his eye. Encourage him to think about how each piece will be used and how long it will last. Talk about where it might have come from.

Expose your kids to a world of fabric and sheets beyond bed-in-a-bag. If they have an interest, help them find a way to learn to sew. There are classes almost everywhere, but there are also people willing to teach a new generation about sewing, and lots of nearly free sewing machines are available on Craigslist.

ALLOW FOR SELF-EXPRESSION

Consider all the possibilities for freedom of expression. Encourage your teen to find art that interests her and to find out about the artist and the medium. Perhaps she'd like to use her own art—one better.

Teens like to exist inside living 3-D scrapbooks, with their passions, peers, and experiences swimming in imagery all around them. Set up the rules ahead of time for what isn't allowed on the walls. There are a lot of different materials that can enhance self-expression. Corkboard-covered walls are an ideal method for capturing everything a teen wants to see on her wall. Sheets of cork *flooring* work best for this and can be sourced in big sheets at Home Depot. They can be painted easily and either nailed or liquid-nailed to the wall. One of my favorite self-expression inviters is Idea Paint, which creates a whiteboard-like finish on any wall. You can buy a clear version, which goes over any color, or white. Let your teen scribble and write his passions away, engulfing himself in his own graffiti. The best part of this is that it's erasable, and you can maintain erasing power if anything is offensive to you. Establish what is offensive during the paint job.

You can also hang thin metal craft wire horizontally across a wall and invite your child to do some old-school display of images by fastening them across the wire with clothespins. There is something interesting about horizontal rows, perhaps a series of these wire lines (hung high), with stuff clipped to them; it literally and figuratively elevates concert tickets, pictures, and postcards to a form of sculpture. A wall of magnetic paint is another great way to create a wall-sized mural of keepsakes and other ephemera from your teen's life career and can also be written on with chalk.

MANAGING MESS

Now, what about the mess? So many parents of teens I've worked with bemoan the teenage motif of "slob chic"—clothes and papers piled or tossed about, making it impossible to find anything important without a lot of frustration. Teenagers are old enough to keep their spaces orderly and to manage the inflow of clean clothes and outflow of dirty laundry, yet the business of being a teenager, perhaps the hormones alone, completely disables this skill for many. This is not a design issue as much as a diplomatic one, and it can be managed by creating understanding and a workable organizational system.

For some teens, the piles seem to be a wholesale rejection of closets, drawers, hangers, and hampers, with a strong preference for the floor. Instead of fighting this, perhaps a floor-based system of clothing organization would solve much of this problem. Score a series of enormous bins, the likes of which may contain sports equipment for school, with ample and oversized signage (such as *CLEAN, DIRTY, T-SHIRTS, UNIFORMS, PJS*) to keep clothing sorted, if not organized. The problem with messy piles, aside from their ugliness and the irritation that comes from an unused chest of drawers or expensive closet system, is that the piles make it difficult to find anything, to get ready for school, and to know what's there. Ginormous bins and obvious signage are a great accommodation to teenage sloth, yes, but they're also a system that reduces the "Mom! I can't find XYZ shirt/pants/homework!" self-induced hysteria that accompanies piles syndrome. Furthermore, this floor system agrees with a child used to throwing balls into hoops wherever she is—making sport of the piles.

The teenage experience is a swift seven years. Spending a ton of money on furniture or built-ins that can't be passed on or appreciated once your teen becomes a college student doesn't make sense. Don't feel bad if an extravagant teen environment isn't in your economic reality. Focus on the walls and make changes that, even if they are not your first choice, aren't permanent.

> *It takes courage to grow up and become who you really are.*
>
> —E. E. CUMMINGS

Tell your teenager that he gets to be the design professional. Have him create a floor plan with accurate measurements. Ask him to consider what works and what doesn't with what he has now. Decide on a total budget and stick to it.

Teens, often early adopters of technology, will love the opportunity to dive into Web-tools for their room. Pinterest and tumblr abound with sweet teen room ideas. And by *sweet,* I mean "awesome," as my pre-preteen just informed me. Encourage your teen to recognize her needs first, consider what her room provides next, then the budget, and the images online last. Looking at beautiful rooms without doing the homework first can lead to disappointment for even the most realistic among us. There are also lots of tools online for creating custom wall decals, wallpaper, and even fabric using digital art. Encourage the creative process and self-expression in a positive way, and you might just be thrilled to see burgeoning design skills in your teenager. Teach her to present her ideas to you, with how much everything will cost. Even if you hate everything she'd like to do in her room, have her explain her reasons for choosing that shade of orange or this particular chandelier. Having your teen explain her choices rather than just asking you to buy things may help you find middle ground on the things that don't work for you. You can also inform her that this is how real designers work—they have to work hard to make clients comfortable with their ideas at times.

30

OUTDO YOURSELF OUTSIDE

*Don't forget to stamp your personality
on the outside of your home and in
your yard too.*

Does your house say, "Welcome home! Come inside and be who
you are. I'm yours, I reflect you and what you love!" Even from the
outside, this is not only possible, but important in getting to true
house love. Blending colors and textures you love, how you'll use
the space, and what your house offers is the recipe for good curb
appeal. The big components are tidiness, color, landscaping, and
extras—each category is chock-full of DIY and affordable options
for big change.

MAINTENANCE AND TIDINESS

Keeping everything neat and clean is not all you have to do to
have an attractive exterior, but it is the foundation. You can have
the most gorgeous house and landscaping in the neighborhood,
but if it's not cared for, it quickly announces, "No one lives here,"
or at least "No one cares." If you can afford nothing else, keep your
grass trimmed and the exterior of your home clean, and remove
anything in disrepair. If it's rusty, paint it or remove it, whether
it's a fence or a mailbox. If it's broken, replace it or remove it,
especially if it's a lighting fixture or a gutter. It's hard to love your

house if you struggle to get in at night because you can't see. It's also a monumental bummer if something that's an exterior eyesore (like a broken or overfilled gutter) turns into an interior problem when it fails to divert water away from your foundation and you have inches of water in your basement.

COLOR

Don't limit yourself to the most common house colors as your only choices. A world of tan and white houses is boring, but white and tan houses with teal doors, yellow shutters, black trim, or other bold color schemes are fabulous. If you want to change all the colors, keep proportion in mind: the front door is the star, the shutters or trim are the supporting players, and the siding or cladding is the background. Your front door color should be daring and bold, the shutters, if you have them, need a color that works well but doesn't compete with the door in brightness or boldness.

Picking paint colors for the exterior is different than choosing interior colors. The lighting is profoundly different, and depending on your home and the property surrounding it, you can experience the color from a much greater distance than you can with a wall that's inside your house. If you're struggling, paint a piece of poster board in your intended color and tape it to your house, then walk across the street. Don't choose outdoor colors while standing five feet away.

Color also comes in the form of plants, flowers, outdoor art, house number plaques, lighting, fencing, and anything else that lives outside. You don't need to stick to some hard-and-fast rule about what colors to use and not use, but be choosy about anything that lives outside and becomes part of your overall curb appeal.

LANDSCAPING

Learn about what's best for your yard and about the horticultural hand you've been dealt with respect to trees, shrubs, and soil on your property. Don't forget to learn about what you like. What plants are you drawn to? What shapes do you find pretty? What kind of garden do you want to look at from each window or your patio? The land around your home is yet another opportunity, not only to learn but to create more space that's tailor-made for you.

Before you buy a single plant, consider what you're willing to do for it. If all you want to do is dig a hole, cover it with dirt, and leave it, there are plants that will survive that kind of commitment. Think about variety, not only in color but also in height and overall plant shape, leaf shape and size, and seasonality (when things sprout and bloom).

Smaller houses do better with simpler schemes, including fewer kinds of plants and fewer sizes of plants. Larger homes can absorb and support a scheme with multiple kinds of trees and plants and essentially lots to look at. Do not be afraid to use many of one or two kinds of plants. Wildly varied and multitextural (very hard to maintain) landscapes are costly and unnecessary unless you live to garden or live on a very large property. If your maintenance tolerance is low, your property is small, and your budget is limited, stand firm on two to three types of plants maximum for the front of the house.

Curating a property takes years, even if you have enough money to professionally landscape every square inch today. Plants take time to mature, and it takes a while to learn about the conditions of the land that surrounds your house so you can plant things that will thrive. Take your time.

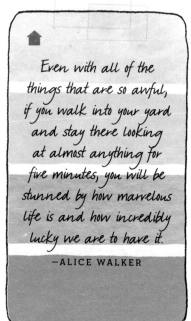

Even with all of the things that are so awful, if you walk into your yard and stay there looking at almost anything for five minutes, you will be stunned by how marvelous life is and how incredibly lucky we are to have it.

—ALICE WALKER

EXTRAS ON THE FACADE— START WITH THE NUMBERS

I love fonts, as many designers do, and the house number presents an affordable way to express yourself with whatever you want: whimsy, formality, your love of nature, even your travels. There are thousands of fonts and hundreds of different ways to express your house number. I am fond of plaques—search Etsy.com for one that speaks to you. I also love stand-alone numbers, now available in three-dimensional forms, as opposed to the standard flat-black numbers of yesterday. Do your best to look beyond the limiting and boring choices offered by Home Depot. You usually only do the house number thing once, so make it count! And make it visible from the street.

LIGHTING UP THE NIGHT

Exterior lighting has a slightly different function than interior lighting. The outside variety must highlight certain aspects of your home and act as a beacon to both visitors and residents alike. It must say, "Walk this way, enter here. Here is where you are." Don't be limited to what your neighbors use, even if they have the exact same home—especially if they have the exact same home. Aim for maximum contrast, think black iron on white or brass against dark green. You'll need to see the light itself, and it's nice to see the fixture from the street.

If you are choosing a pendant for over your door or a wall sconce for beside your door, check out the dimensions of something you like, and create some sort of dummy that you can hold up in the place the light will be installed. The dummy need not be exact—you can use a box, a large can of beans, a bowl, or whatever is approximate—but this will give you an idea of the space your light will fill. Step back, take a look from the other side of the street, and see how you feel about the scale of the light you are considering. Smaller, more diminutive (but not necessarily simpler or more boring) lights work better on small houses. Bigger houses call for bigger fixtures and often more of them. This trick works inside too.

YOU'VE GOT MAIL

If you have to have a mailbox, why not have one that reflects you? Your lush and colorful garden, your whimsical house numbers, your sparkling satin nickel lighting fixtures—it's all about achieving specificity. As an example, you could choose a bright red mailbox, assuming this works with the rest of the colors on your exterior. The point here is not to push red or anything else but to encourage you to explore your options and connect the dots with the other choices you've already made. A mailbox is one of those things you probably won't buy again for a while, so buy something you'll enjoy looking at, something that says, "I am a pleasure to visit whether I'm holding Christmas cards or bills."

MORE THAN A DOORKNOB

What does your front doorknob or door handle look like?
What about your knocker, if you have one? Is it rusty, old, and
nondescript? If you are not up for painting your front door, get
yourself some better door hardware. It doesn't take a fortune,
although putting good quality into your door, the membrane
between you and the outside world, including potential intruders,
isn't the worst idea. The key here is to keep everything in good
working order, tightly fastened, clean, and pleasing to your eyes.
Ideally you'll choose a metal finish with good contrast to the door
color that works with your lighting fixtures, mailbox, and house
numbers.

QUALITY CAUTION

Whenever you buy anything for the exterior of your home, you're
buying something that will go into battle with rain, bird poop,
global warming, burrowing bees, errant baseballs, you name it. It all
takes a beating outside. Buy good quality. Wait if you can't afford it.
Don't buy junk, and don't buy things that don't review well online
or are not reviewed at all for their outdoor hardiness. As I said in
the beginning, everyone seems to be thinking about outdoor living,
and manufacturers are chomping at the bit to sell you more things
for the outside of your house. If you live in Southern California, you
probably have to worry a bit less than I do, living in the Northeast.
Still, buy proven outdoor-weather goods, and they'll make you
smile for longer, which is certainly the goal.

The next time you go out, take your Home Book with you. When you come home, park in front of your house and look at it from the car. What do you notice first? Is it pleasing to you? If so, can you augment or build on the element you like? If it's the flowerpots you see first, can you add more? If the front door color speaks to you, can you add an accessory in the same or a complementary color somewhere else? As long as it's not the front door or something you need for safety, can you take what bugs you the most down or off or out?

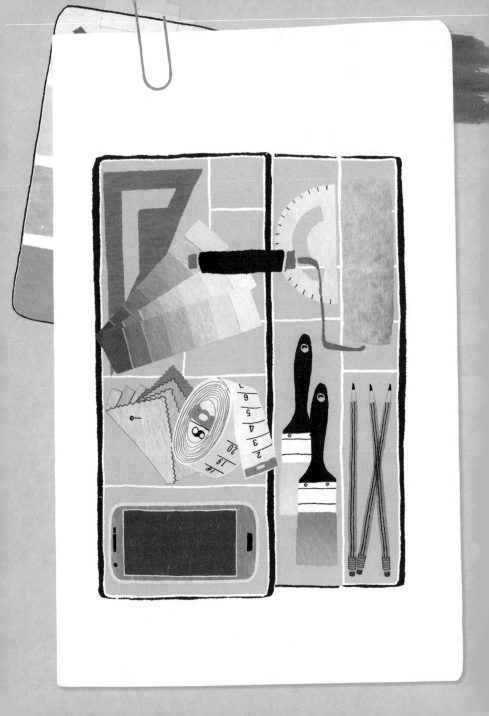

Part Five

SKILLS YOU WILL USE

I hope you are brimming with confidence at this point. It's now time to arm yourself with the key skills that will help you put everything together like an expert who knows you inside and out. Learning how to choose a light fixture or pick a paint color isn't as hard now that you're clear on who you are and the story you're endeavoring to tell within your walls. There is work to be done, and I hope you enjoy it. Some people love working on their homes, and some see it as drudgery—the more you can find to enjoy, the better the outcome will be. The people I've met who really love their homes also really love making improvements, getting their hands dirty, searching for good stuff, and seeing the progress little by little.

I found I could say things
with colors that I could not say
in any other way, things for
which I had no words.

—GEORGIA O'KEEFFE

31

USING COLOR WITH SMARTS

Pick colors like a pro throughout your home.

Color isn't what you think it is. Color is actually a sensory, neurological experience. More simply, it is created when our eyes, brain, and available light work together. Since everyone's eyes and brain are different, and since the light in life is always changing, color is always changing and looks different to different people. Beyond the mechanics, how we see color is also deeply personal, influenced by our memories as well as our native culture.

Linda Holtzschue explains it this way in her book, *Understanding Color*:

Everyone has experienced buying an article of clothing and arriving home to find that it is a different color than it seemed to be in the store or selecting a paint color and being astonished at the final result. Even the idea of color is unstable. A number of people looking at the same thing often disagree about exactly what the color is. . . . The instability of color has a number of causes. The first of these is the way in which colors are generated by light, reflected from surfaces, and sensed by the human eye. The color of an object is no more permanent or absolute than the light by which it is seen.

When you are choosing colors, test a possible color alongside what's already in the room—the givens as opposed to another possible color. Never hold your two top choices side by side. Each option, when placed together, will affect how you see the other, an effect that is gone when they stand alone. Never choose paint colors inside a paint store, fabric in a fabric store, or anything in any store, if you can help it. The best place to make a decision about color is the exact location where the proposed color will be experienced in your home. Not only will color look different with the light sources and neighboring colors in your home (walls, flooring, furniture), but retail environments are typically lit with fluorescent lighting, a cheap, low-heat-emitting source that creates cooler-toned light. This means that most colors appear cooler or bluer—or at the very least, different—in stores than they will appear in your home with natural or traditional incandescent lighting.

Spend time thinking about colors you are drawn to, before you're in paint chip decision mode. Our preferences for colors are undoubtedly related to our personal experience, our subconscious memories, and our culture. Cultures around the world have preferences and long-held ideas about the hues that quite literally color their societies. As individuals, we develop preferences or distaste for color based on associations that we may not even remember. Holtzschue explains it this way: "Aunt Agatha made you eat broccoli in her pink kitchen; you hate broccoli and pink. Personal experience also determines each person's concept of colors."

Once again, it's all about you, your experience, your story, your wholly unique experience with color. It's up to you to tune out the noise about colors that are fashionable or now passé. And here is the hardest part: it's up to you to let go of what others may think of your color choices—whether they may find your orange kitchen garish or your cream-colored bedroom bland. Everyone brings their own experience and points of reference to their opinions about your color schemes. That's fine, because you're not painting your walls for them; you're doing it for you.

Color can soothe or invigorate. If you have a particular goal in mind for a space, consider the effects of colors on the body. Blues and greens are said to be calming, while reds and oranges are warmer and more energizing. Don't disregard your conscious responses either. If you find certain reds calming and that's the feeling you want in your bedroom, go with red! Perhaps you had a soft red blanket as a child. Color theory is just that—theory. It is up to you to fill in the blanks on what will work in practice and for your life.

WHERE TO LOOK

Look everywhere for color inspiration: the produce aisle, your closet, nature. Don't just look at composed rooms; pay attention to everything that catches your eye, everything that triggers a response to color. Pay attention to graphic design—you may be drawn to certain palettes, or groupings of colors, positioned in close proximity in an advertisement, website, or product packaging. Perhaps this palette can be applied to a room in your house. Use it all.

Put random objects from around the house together to see how their colors work together. I was once working on a 1940s bathroom awash in gray and black. I could not figure out what softer, warmer color to bring in. The black and gray were so harsh and severe, but using something very different, such as pink or yellow, that would give an obvious infusion of warmth didn't work. So I started just placing things in different hues around the bathroom. I tossed in a cream-colored scarf, a red napkin, a sandy tan-colored box of tissues. Eureka! The tan worked perfectly with the gray and black and reminded me of how neutrals—more specifically, hues from nature—tend to take the bite out of rooms that are too cool or too warm. So I painted the walls a pale caramel and used lots of natural textures to achieve a totally different space.

COLOR BOARDS

Assembling a collection of fabric swatches, paint chips, and images of furniture on paper is a time-tested design tool. Sometimes called a vision board, it's the act of clustering representative colors, textures, and shapes for a space on paper so you can see the room abstractly. This tool can be misleading: it's not a diagram or a representation of the actual room; it displays the ingredients. Some things on the board will be dominant, some will be minor—but the relationship between them is not always obvious. Having said that, it's a worthwhile exercise to get a feeling of your room's elements by seeing how they work together on a sheet of paper.

I have an enormous box of fabric swatches and another bin full of paint chips, usually small pieces torn from the longer sheets found on a typical manufacturer's fan deck. I also have samples of flooring, woven shades and blinds, metallic finishes, and tile thrown in to another basket. I like to pick from each basket and assemble a collection of colors, textures, metals, and woods that look interesting together in a loose collage on the floor. Do these elements work well in combination? There is little to no chance I'll be using the actual fabric from the swatch or the paint color from the chip; I'm just playing around to see what works as a starting point for colors.

A PRIMER ON PICKING PAINT COLORS

The question I get most often from friends and relatives is, "How do you pick a paint color?" The options are mystifying, with what seems like hundreds of versions of each color. What people really mean is, "I know I want tan, but which tan?" While there really are only six colors in our world (red, orange, yellow, green, blue, and violet), there are millions of perceptible and nameable colors in our universe. The naming of colors by paint manufacturers can and does have an impact on how you make your selections, even how you see the colors. I always tell people to ignore the names, but it is so hard—especially since they are all taken from the most beautiful landscapes and vacation locales in the world, such as Aspen Green, Nantucket Blue, and Amalfi Pink.

Once you know the color you want in vague terms ("I want to paint my daughter's room pale pink"), go to the paint store and look at the pink options—all of them. Gather up all the chips that include what you think is an attractive pale pink and take them home. Don't try to figure it out standing there in front of a sea of paint chips among other bewildered-looking shoppers trying to do the same thing. When you get home, look at your loot. Notice that some pinks are derived from or near the purples and blues, while others are derived from oranges and reds. (You can tell this easily from the gradient on the chip—pale pink on one end, red on the other.) Consider the source to determine which pinks you like best. Unless your goal is a vibrant color, toss out the three to four darkest or brightest choices right off the bat. The mistake people make most often is choosing a paint color that has too much color in it. Rarely have I heard clients say, "This is too light or subdued," once it's on the wall.

Your next goal is to have approximately three to four options to choose from. Hopefully you don't have more than that, but if you do, don't worry. Don't spend any time with the color chips anywhere else but in the room you intend to paint. Spend a little time holding them in your hand or seeing how they work with the flooring, but soon after that, tape them to a wall surface. Remember, don't tape your options up *next* to each other. Color is experienced as a function of available light as well as the other colors surrounding it. So if you have three pinks, and one has a touch of peach, another has a bluish tone, and the last is a pale creamy pink, these differentiating characteristics will be much more prominent if they are all right next to each other. Choose separate walls altogether to experience the chips. Tape them up and then walk out. I like to live with the chips on my walls for days, looking at them as I pass by, at a distance, in the daytime and at night. Don't force a timeline for this process. Taking a break from it for a day or two will often result in an entirely different perception.

When you think you have a favorite, don't try and explain it or figure it out. It's just your favorite, *which is enough*. Take the others down and leave that one up. Try and incorporate other elements you may use into the room—not right up against the chip, but somewhere near it in your field of vision. For instance, if you have an area rug you plan to use, leave it on the floor and tape the chip a bit closer to the floor, then stand there and experience the two to get a feel for how they work together in the room. Don't look too closely. Don't try to match things up perfectly, and try the squinty technique: tape up a paint chip, walk backward about five to ten paces, and then squint. This is how the color will most often be perceived—as blurry background, not the object of scrutiny.

Once you've picked your color, buy the most expensive paint you can afford. I am cheap to a fault, but not with paint. You end up paying either way. If you buy cheap paint, you'll need more of it, because the cheaper paints generally don't cover as well. If you buy a better paint, you'll use less and work less for a good finish.

Remember that your painted wall will look different once it's completely dry, given a full two coats, in different kinds of lighting, when the room is put back together with furniture and drapes, and so on. If someone else is handling the painting, be around while they're doing the job. If you truly hate the color, it's likely that all the factors I just mentioned (number of coats, lighting, furniture, and so on) won't change your mind. It's best to stop the painting if you're going to switch to a different color. However, if you're simply unsure or uneasy, be patient and don't worry. Wait until the room is put together and you see the color in all kinds of light before you make any decisions about it. It's always darkest before the paint dries.

What Finish to Choose

There are multiple finishes to choose from—flat, eggshell, satin, semigloss, and high gloss are the most common. The finish is the amount of sheen in the paint, and the more sheen, or gloss, the easier it is to wipe down. Sheen also highlights imperfections in your walls, so if you have an old house, flat is a better choice. It's trendy to do high gloss, but only do it if you like it; high gloss is the hardest paint to work with and get a smooth finish. It's de rigueur to put semigloss in kitchens and bathrooms, but it's not essential. Keep in mind that when you are choosing a paint color, it will always appear more vibrant in a semigloss or high-gloss finish.

Green and Yellow—Tough Nuts to Crack

Greens and yellows are the hardest colors to make work. Gray is tough too. Some greens can be too "toothpastey" or remind us of that pallid green look we get when we're about to vomit. Yellow can be too much like pee and not enough like butter, and it's very difficult to ascertain the right yellow from a chip. I like to use sample pots for yellows. Yellow is also more sensitive to light bounce than other colors and can easily come across as too green or too bright, which is tough to foresee from a tiny chip.

YOUR TURN
FIRST, THE ROOM ON PAPER

Do you have a room that needs a color change, but you don't know where to begin? Good. Stay away from the paint store or fan deck and play with colors around you. Start in your closet, at the grocery store, or with what you already own in the house—it doesn't matter. Pick a color or two (no commitment) and create a color board on a flat surface.

1　Once you have a collection of colors and textures you like, glue them together in a collage; don't worry about the arrangement of things, just make sure each thing you chose is visible.

2　If you like what's coming together, keep going, and see what other colors work well with your chosen color. So if you've decided you want your room to be painted a shade of purple, play with what other colors might work well with your purple of choice. (Try yellows, golds, or whatever color is opposite the one you chose on the color wheel.) You may get your answer from a favorite shirt or book cover.

No one is going to come and say, "No, sorry. That doesn't work." Let yourself play and find what you like with this exercise. It will guide you well in working on your space. If you really like your collage of colors from random objects, go to the paint store and choose a few chips and see how they work with everything else. Live with those for a while, then find five viable color options to narrow down the wall color. Toss out the two darkest ones, tape up the rest, and live with them. In a matter of days, you'll have a color that works.

WHAT TO DO IF THE COLOR FEELS WRONG AFTER IT'S ON THE WALLS

1　Relax. This can be fixed.

2　If you're not up for a whole new paint job, consider a 50 percent topcoat. You can take the paint you have left to the paint store and mix the gallons with a gallon of white base. Mix it all up (better yet, have the paint store do it) in a five-gallon bucket.

Usually this takes the sharpness out of a color that's too bright or intense. Just know that once this paint is gone, it will be impossible to reorder or match with a new batch.

3   *Would an accent wall work to counterbalance the offending color? Color has a relationship to its surroundings—if something seems too bright, perhaps a bright element or accent wall will take some of the bite out of the color that isn't quite working.*

4   *Patterns, stencils, and framed art trump any offensive wall color. Think about how the color you dislike could work as a background for a stenciled design, mural, or gallery wall.*

5   *Just do it—repaint. It's inevitable for all of us at some point; covering a color that didn't turn out well with fresh paint is what must be done. If you do feel you've made a bad choice, take care in considering what you want in the new color: Was the original color too cool? Too warm? Too much like Grandma's house? Pay attention to your response—it will help you to make a better choice next time.*

YES, YOUR WALLS CAN TALK

Maximize your largest palette
for self-expression.

Unless you live in a glass house, you have more wall space to fill than you have floor space to furnish, ceiling space to gaze at, or windows to dress. Treat each wall in your house as an opportunity to shape an experience—to make someone feel or think something. Walls are your biggest, least expensive opportunity to say something unique in your home.

Although you may paint all the walls in a room the same color, you may decide to treat them differently in terms of what you hang or don't hang. Each wall is a distinct palette for expression. Think of your walls the way you may already think of your tabletops or mantels—walls need balance, contrast, variety, and editing. Even if you leave a wall blank, or hang just one painting, do this with purpose. Here are some ideas for composing interesting walls that speak to you.

FEATURE WALLS

Be on the lookout for feature walls. These are walls that you can see from a distance or are wider, taller, or framed walls defined by an opening or a doorway on an opposing wall. They may have an interesting feature such as a fireplace or an interesting-shaped window embedded in them. Feature-wall candidates have something you'd like to highlight, or may be plain where you want to do something big. Just make sure it's a wall you can enjoy by walking by or sitting in front of it. Feature walls are no fun if they are tucked away. Once you've identified which walls can be featured in some way, consider a bolder or more whimsical wall color, stenciled pattern, eye-catching wall paper, mural, or meaningful collection to be showcased. Don't be afraid to use that giant piece of artwork, or a large-print wallpaper. A feature wall is a bit like an oversized canvas.

GALLERY WALLS

Gallery walls of family photos, dutifully printed in black and white and framed accordingly, have become very popular. This is a great device. I love groups of things. But gallery walls don't always work. There are only two rules. One, hang only what you love. Hanging art or photographs that speak to you, make you smile, or warm your heart—nothing else. The subject can be someone you love or someone you don't even know, in the case of art photography, but you have to have some sort of positive emotional response to what you hang on your walls. They are there to work, not just look pretty.

Two, follow the five-foot rule. This relates to how far away you are most often when experiencing the photos or framed art. Smaller pieces with lots of intricate detail, including small faces about an inch tall in the photograph, are best experienced while standing about five feet away or less. Perhaps they would work for an entry wall in a tight foyer, a hallway, or an intimate spot in the bedroom. Small pieces and small faces don't work for walls that you see within a large room from more than five feet away. Those walls call for bigger compositions and bigger faces.

Gallery walls are great, but choose your locations carefully. I worked on an apartment in New York where we installed a twelve-foot-tall gallery wall with hundreds of framed photos, some no bigger than four-by-six inches, in a very narrow foyer with high ceilings. It worked because people walked right by the wall and could see everything—all the detail, all the fun faces—right in front of them. Although a larger piece of art could have worked there due to the sheer square footage the wall offered, it was too tight of a space to fully experience something large. Last, gallery walls work when something ties each framed piece together—all the

> *Design is a plan for arranging elements in such a way as best to accomplish a particular purpose.*
>
> —CHARLES EAMES

same size frame, same color frame, same subject, or when the whole collection of framed pieces are altogether different. The two opposite approaches are equally great: order and similarity or mish-mashed miscellany.

USING THE WHOLE WALL AND THE "WHITE" SPACE

I use the full expanse of my walls, and because I'm six feet tall, I'm partial to the top half. I hang high shelves 12 inches from the ceiling as both an aesthetic choice and a device for keeping stuff out of my children's reach. I also like using the whole wall for framed art and pictures, whether I'm working with "high ceilings" or not. The key is to manage the white space, or whatever space surrounds the framed art and pictures. "White space" is a graphic design term that refers to the space outside of text or graphics in color—the space behind the central features in a design. When you are composing a wall, choose order or randomness when it comes to spacing and arranging things. Making them tight and orderly is nice because it leaves a lot of blank wall space outside the tight and orderly frames. If you spread them out, you get wall space in between. You can map it all out on the floor or wing it by hanging one, then hanging another close to it, and putting the arrangement together like a puzzle, until the wall is mostly covered. Don't be afraid to use the full height of your space.

FUNCTIONAL ELEMENTS

Don't forget that walls can be workhorses, just like furniture. Coat hooks, wine bottle racks, picture ledges, shelving, and plate hangers all serve to make the walls work, either as three-dimensional art, storage, or a way to keep stuff off of other surfaces. Don't be afraid to go big here—a full wall of shelving, from floor to ceiling, is striking; a row or cluster of hooks in an interesting shape (heart, star, peace sign) is nice to look at whether they are in use or not.

TEXTURE

Just as you can add color to any wall, you can apply texture in many ways. You may want to use clay, stucco, or a stone veneer. You can also use reclaimed wood with a product like Stikwood. You can also use beadboard, wainscoting, tile, pressed tin, or latticework. Think about qualities or adjectives you're trying to bring into the space.

PATTERN

Stencils are a fabulous technique for expressing pattern in an inexpensive and unique way. They can give you what wallpaper provides at a fraction of the cost. And you can do an allover pattern or just center one interesting design on the wall. Think about the kinds of patterns that would connect to your story—Art Deco? woodland? brocade? geometric? toile? If you can think of it, someone can make a stencil out of it, if they haven't already. Check Etsy.com for great stencil makers and tutorials.

Traditional wallpaper or self-stick wallpaper are great options too, but they will be pricier. If you find a paper you love, consider covering just one wall, such as the one your bed rests against, to make an exaggerated headboard. Or the wall that faces your front door as an entry hello. Or the wall behind your couch. Stripes are delightful in any direction and any width. They even come in a self-stick option: see wallsneedlove.com.

CREATE OFF-THE-WALL VIGNETTES

Beyond what you can put *on* the wall, also consider displays that you can put *against* the wall. Your wall color and a favorite statue, vase, trophy, or bookend with an interesting silhouette can work together to build a vignette that highlights the shapes and contours of the items against your wall color. People struggle with composing artful shelves or tabletops, forgetting that the backdrop is the first element of the vignette. Shelving without a back panel illustrates this well. The items on the shelf pop if they contrast with the wall and the color peeks through. You can always paint just a portion of the wall. For example, you can paint the space above your fireplace mantel a color to effect contrast with what you want to use on the mantel. Make changes that highlight what you already love.

My mom, an award-winning, retired educator, told me awhile ago that children who live within walls covered in maps absorb the geographic information without even knowing it. I don't know if there is science to back this up, but I believe it. I trust that our walls affect us whether we like it or not, so why not artfully manage what you and your loved ones absorb every single day via your walls? Whether it's a happy color, an emotive artwork, a whimsical wallpaper, an intricate geometric stencil, family history, or all of the above, walls are yours to use for beauty and benefit.

Find the most boring wall in your house—one that's tucked away in a corner or behind an often-open door doesn't count. Choose a wall that you see often, one that has some prominence. Take everything off this wall and give it some room to breathe. See it empty and blank for a few days. Then ask yourself these questions: Based on what's around it, what does this wall need? Does it need words? Faces? Color? Structure? Texture? Does it need one big statement or lots of small things to make it interesting?

If you have absolutely no idea what to do with the wall and the preceding questions make your head spin, choose an interesting color, one you really like, from something in an *adjacent* room (the teal in a throw pillow, the gold in a picture frame, the dark gray in the stone flooring), and paint the boring wall that interesting color. Don't decide anything else until the paint is dry. The answer of what next will probably come. What contrasts with the color? Play with objects and art held up against your new wall. This is play. Enjoy it. The result will be better if you do one thing at a time and compose your artful wall without pressure.

33

GO BOLD

These are the projects and spaces where you can unleash your bold (everyone has it).

There is a correlation between confidence and boldness. The house-confident among us easily find places they can be bold—not just with colors, but also with prints, textures, scale, and self-expression. Being bold means taking chances and using something you really love, even if it's not what your mother did, what your neighbor does, or what you've been taught is acceptable. (This isn't your mother's or your neighbor's house.)

Lots of people dream of raspberry or teal rooms, bright green couches, big-printed wallpapers, but don't feel they can pull off anything so daring. This stems from the fear of doing something wrong or doing something that is "too much." If this describes you, start with baby steps. Going bold is hard for the uninitiated. Start with bold choices and projects that aren't expensive in spaces that are begging for a bold statement.

POWDER ROOMS

Powder rooms can be jewel boxes, offering a brief, solitary encounter to visitors in an interesting and unique space. I like bright, bold colors and wallpaper, whimsy and interesting things to look at, even in the smallest powder rooms. Why not? These rooms are often small and not used for any function beyond the toilet and sink. No need to pay attention to perfect lighting for makeup application or concern yourself with trying to make it appear bigger with lighter colors. Paint the entire space in a color you find fabulous and interesting, dark and dramatic, or bright and cheery—take a chance. It probably has little natural light and little wall space in general. Regardless, use the color you've been longing to try. Wallpaper is a great option for powder rooms as well, since they likely require a small number of rolls, making it an inexpensive boldness, even with pricey paper. Wallpapers that would be overwhelming or too much to look at in a room that you sleep in are perfectly suited for a room in which you're spending five to ten minutes at a time by yourself. Who doesn't want something interesting to look at while in the john?

DINING ROOMS

Dining rooms, especially the formal variety, are my second favorite spot for a bold statement. If it's a space you use every day or an open dining space, it won't have the same punch. But a self-contained dining room used for family dinners, parties, or festive times is an ideal place for a bold statement on your walls. Try a color you love in high gloss. Try wallpaper. Try stripes. Try something you wouldn't feel comfortable trying elsewhere. In the dining room, it's OK.

If you have a fairly muted palette throughout your home, perhaps there is a darker color from a work of art or fabric that you can use in your dining room. If you have tan and pale blue elsewhere, a navy dining room rocks. If you have grays and pale yellow, why not a slate or black dining room? If you have sage greens and cream throughout your house, why not forest green walls or metallic wallpaper? The dining room is a place for spectacle and social time, two human experiences best enveloped by bold color.

If you're not up for a bold color, why not a bold light fixture? The dining room table is begging for something audacious above it—something expansive and elegant, or something sleek with sharp corners. If you are afraid of stepping out of standard lighting fixtures for the rest of the house, splurge on the dining room fixture. The dining room is also the space for wholly impractical furniture—absurdly high-backed chairs or glass pedestal tables. The dining room is not a place to lounge, and most often it's seen empty. Feel free to use furniture that, when left unused, has striking silhouettes, like sculpture.

ENTRYWAYS

How about a bold color as a tone-setter for the rest of your house? Some entryways are defined and small, not unlike a large powder room. They are a pass-through space, not a place in which to linger, and they are ideal for the use of statement colors. You may not want to sleep inside four magenta walls, but walking through them is divine. The idea of sculpture furniture works here too.

ACCENT WALL

I prescribe accent walls sparingly, let me get that on the table. Sometimes people use accent walls because they're "trying out" a color. Accent walls are not about the background color, they are about what's being accented or contrasted in front of the wall color. The best accent walls are those that stand alone, independent in some way, or those that house important furniture. For instance, a bold accent wall can beef up your headboard and make the whole wall a statement for your bedroom. Accent walls work nicely in entryways. Walls that contain an interesting vignette of artwork and decor that you love make good accent walls, especially if there is a relationship between the art and the wall color. But if you're doing an accent wall because you are afraid of painting the whole room in your desired color—be bold! Or split the difference and find a color that you can live with on four walls.

BE BOLD ELSEWHERE IN OTHER WAYS

Has anyone ever told you, "You can only use large-scale art in a big house"? Or, "You can only paint large rooms dark colors"? Maybe someone stated categorically, "You can only use big prints in small doses," or "You should choose neutrals for your bigger furniture and pieces you're likely to have for a long time." Ever hear any of those? I'm sure these people meant well. They didn't want you to make a mistake. They, too, thought there were big mistakes to be made if you do something against some arcane decorating code. The truth is, interesting trumps scale and the rules for scale. Paint a room an interesting color, connect it to other features in your home, and I don't care how small your house is, it will work. Use a large-scale artwork that makes you feel good. No matter how small your house is, it will work. If you are concerned that a print is too bold for a chair or sofa, try a large swatch on it, which you may have to pay for, and see how you feel. Even small rooms can contain big, bold prints, especially if those prints are the focus of the room, the statement, the art to be experienced by whoever is in the space. Small houses are great laboratories for big things. Don't feel limited by the size of your home. Let what is interesting to you triumph over what others have told you is not wise because of the size of your house.

If you're afraid of making a mistake and are hiding in safe choices for your home—neutral colors, concepts you see everywhere, a general blandness—ask yourself what you're afraid of. Who do you think will judge you for making a choice that is outside of what you see in your friends' and relatives' homes? What will happen if you choose something that is different, even strange, and love it? Why do you need to make choices that are safe as opposed to choices that feel more daring? Try out these questions in your Home Book:

1   *If you knew that no one would judge you and that you would love it, what color would you paint one room in your house?*

2   *If you knew there would be no negative repercussions and that you would love it, what would you put in your house that may be an unconventional choice for you?*

3   *What color makes you happiest?*

4   *What giant thing do you wish you had in your house?*

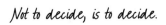

Not to decide, is to decide.

—HARVEY G. COX
(AND A FAVORITE
OF MY FATHER-IN-LAW,
FRANK RIENZO)

34

DON'T *BE* NEUTRAL, *CHOOSE* NEUTRALS

*Determine whether your zest for
neutrals is a genuine desire or a
safe haven from color.*

Don't choose the tan, taupe, and cream room because you can't
decide on which kind of blue works for you. Don't choose white
because you can't figure out anything else. Having said that, there
is nothing inherently wrong with neutrals. They do not have to be
boring or safe or bland, just as beaches, desert landscapes, and
wood aren't boring or bland. If you are using a neutral palette
because you find neutrals soothing, you prefer the focus on textures
and natural materials, or you feel there is something freeing and
clean about them, then by all means go neutral.

Neutrals are usually quieter. They make a calm collective
statement. You pay more attention to variation and detail when you
are in a room swathed in neutrals. However, if there is no detail, no
eye-catching features, then the room is just blah. If you've chosen
neutrals because you are afraid, then you'll miss the opportunity to
feature key art, decor, and details. A room can be too quiet.

A dear friend of mine, Nancy Mayorga, weaves all sorts of metals
and textures into her neutral and white-bathed spaces with delightful
results. I clearly remember her artwork, sculpture, and decorative
items, back-dropped by white couches. Her gold-and-black horse
sculpture (she is an equestrian) is the main event in her white living

room. This is even more impressive to behold than her daring to have white upholstery with a young child and animals underfoot.

If you are someone who feels you can only buy in the tan, beige, cream, and sand territories of furniture, paint colors, or fabrics, ask yourself why you desire a neutral room. Do you wear a lot of neutrals? Do you love nature? I don't question your reasons—I want *you* to. If you are choosing something because you don't know what else to do, think about your closet, your favorite foods, beloved photos, anything in life that grabs your eye. However, if you sincerely get giddy at the thought of blending six shades of beige in a cream-colored room with lots of wood, let's do it. Paint your neutral story with a passion!

CONSIDER THE FOCUS OF THE ROOM

What is the focus of the space? Do you have a gorgeous piece of art that you want to showcase? Do you have a wood, stone, or metal element that can command the focus of the room? Think about something bold but colorless that can be the focus. Also consider mirrors, plants, wood, metal, art, and textiles.

TEXTURE IS YOUR FRIEND

A neutral-clad room is the best environment to showcase textures. Think about fuzzy, nubby, smooth, woven, or silky textiles. Fabrics offer the most obvious opportunities to showcase texture, but they are not the only game in town. Think about rough-hewn, burly, smooth, and stained woods. Metals and metalwork. Sculpture, glasswork, and pottery. I firmly believe there should be something soft and fuzzy, as well as something cool and smooth, in each room. Humans like to touch things, and rooms are not just for the eyes. Texture also plays with colors and how they are presented, so you can have a series of whites in different textured fabrics that read very differently and provide something visually stirring. Although they're not technically textures as much as effects, mirrors, high-gloss surfaces, and reflective surfaces do almost the same thing—add dimension without color. In addition to the fuzzy, don't forget the shiny.

USE THE SURGICAL COLOR STRIKE

Small doses of color have a big impact in a neutral room. Select something you love and use it sparingly. Think about art, blankets, books, picture frames, pillows, flowers, plants, and glass. I am not fond of the overused expression "just for a pop of color." However, since color does actually burst forth when our eye experiences a general absence of color, it applies here.

CONSIDER BLACK AND GRAY

Gray is a great neutral that offers a wider range of choices, believe it or not, than a standard beige or tan, which is a bit more limited. Gray works with just about everything, even yellow. Consider black, too, as a great neutral ally, especially when you use a lot of white. A little bit of cast-iron detailing or a black-piped pillow can be great in a neutral room.

Neutrals are rooms you can work on forever. Without the yoke of trying to match colors, which people never seem to want to give up, you can always find and use a range of timeless woven products, wood features, and objects from nature that will work in your space. The biggest challenge is to make it *your* neutral room. Remember to keep it personal, and don't just put out a series of baskets and shells because they work with the color palette. Find the aspects of neutral that speak to you, what environments or materials or images inspire you. Neutral is not a universal concept—it's what you make of it, and it's at its best when it's connected to you.

If your desire is to go all neutral, the first step is to get clear on why you're drawn to all these colors from nature. Where does the inspiration to use neutrals come from? The beach? The desert? Sunlight? Wood? Memories of your mom in a tan sweater? Uncover the source of your desire for a neutral palette, and then make it personal and alive. Here are some questions to uncover your neutral story:

1   *What is your favorite natural environment?*

2   *Do you have a particular memory of being there or seeing this environment?*

3   *Do you have actual artifacts or things from this environment you can use as a catalyst for your space?*

4   *What are the colors and textures of your favorite natural environment? You may find that some Internet browsing helps this answer along; photographs of Montauk or the desert in Arizona or the Maine coast could help fill in the blanks. What other colors and textures are prominent? Can you use these in your neutral-hued room? Can you use water to go with the sand? The green lakeside foliage? The red rocks?*

35

SOURCING LIKE A PRO

*Decide what to spend some money
on and what to buy inexpensively
or get for free.*

At one time, designers and decorators had exclusive to-the-trade-only access to a lot of high-end furniture, wallpaper, and fabrics that could not be purchased directly by consumers. Shortly after the year 2000, this started to change. "To the trade" still exists, but it is diminishing. This change, while making many things less exclusive, means you have far more options than just the big furniture stores where you live, and much of it is online.

The Internet has driven the consumer sourcing process for the home through websites like Houzz and Pinterest. The flood of images, options, prices, and clock-ticking on sales can make anyone crazy. Whether you can afford to shop without looking at price tags or you're curating your home exclusively from hand-me-downs and garage sales, buy what you love and only those things that won't give you heartburn afterward. Here are some thoughts on how to source and make decisions as if someone were paying you to do it.

LEARN THE MARKET

A knowledge of suppliers in nearly every category for the home may be the greatest asset a designer has. A good designer knows about the guy in New Hampshire who makes sinks out of seashells and the guy in Texas who makes bar stools out of horseshoes. The designer knows the woman who makes the best slipcovers and the fabric, made in Germany, that can go in the machine but looks like leather and is made of recycled water bottles. Take a look at the sources section of your favorite home magazine to introduce yourself to a few new brands. Get a sense of what's high-end, what's middle of the road, what's just plain cheap. Read about custom-made pieces and European brands. Don't mistake *shopping* for learning the market—you're seeing what's out there, getting a sense of trends, deciding what you like, and getting a feel for price points.

PRETEND IT'S SOMEONE ELSE'S MONEY

Professional designers and decorators are detached. They create options they hope will be right for whoever has hired them, but they are not weighed down by any kind of fear, desperation, or urgency. They see the budget as a range, and they are not afraid to skirt around the edges for the right aesthetic choice. The right piece is the ultimate goal. Pretending you're a designer for someone else gives you the freedom to look at options way out of your price range and consider them, so you can hopefully find a less expensive option or find room in the budget elsewhere for something perfect but more expensive than you planned for. In all cases, consider the small-medium-large options with regard to cost. What is the high-end version, the budget version, and the in-between version of what you are looking for? Last, treat the creation of your space as art and design, a professional project where you've been chosen—this attitude changes everything.

WHERE AND WHEN TO LOOK

You probably have stores you prefer or catalogs you think are interesting. Look well beyond what's familiar to or comfortable for you. Most big furniture retailers have a significant markup to work with and many sales events throughout the year. It helps not to be in a hurry.

Stay blind to the labels different retailers or manufacturers put on their products. Be open to the entire line of options at stores that offer a range of goods in many categories, and consider stores and online retailers that you've already decided are too modern, too traditional, or too formal/informal. Look at websites you may find to be too expensive too. Even if you want your house to look like something out of *Dwell* magazine, see what Pottery Barn has. Even if you think modern design is cold and heartless, go to West Elm, Crate & Barrel, Room and Board, and others that might have what you consider modern or transitional fare. Even if you think it's out of your range, look at Serena & Lily, Wisteria, and Horchow. Look at Target and JC Penney. This is like dating—be open, and don't sell yourself short or be a snob. One of my favorite quotes supports this approach. Pablo Picasso said, "Inspiration exists, but it has to find you working." The work here is the soul searching paired with searching the market.

BRING YOUR TOOLS

Take the room, or at least the measurements and your ideas for it, with you when you shop, whether online or in stores. This is not to match things up, but to remind you of your intentions and goals for the space, as well as the given parameters. On your body, where colors comingle in closer proximity, matching has its place. But in a room, the colors swirl in space with natural and artificial light,

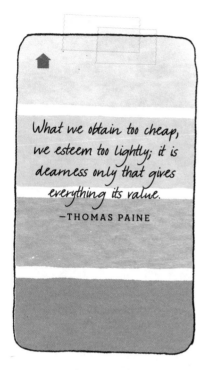

> What we obtain too cheap,
> we esteem too lightly; it is
> dearness only that gives
> everything its value.
>
> —THOMAS PAINE

shadow, and other things that make the colors appear different throughout the day. Bring your stuff to remind you of the direction you're going. It also just helps to have all your measurements close at hand.

CONTRAST COLOR, TEXTURE, AND SCALE

Designers create a composition for a room by balancing light, dark, masculine, feminine, formal, and informal. There are times that we willingly tip the balance and have a distinctly feminine room or a distinctly dark room, but a little bit of the opposite always works and keeps the room from looking too formulaic. Also consider contrasting shapes. If every object in your space is sharp, squared off, and angular, the space will feel severe and austere, even a little cold. Bring curves and organic shapes in somewhere. The same holds true for a room full of curves and billowy forms; something tapered or angular, sometimes referred to as "clean-lined," will do well to balance all the round edges. It's difficult to achieve this balance while shopping at one store or even three. A well-composed room always starts in the mind, is not swayed by what's on (or missing from) shelves, and draws from multiple sources.

BE AWARE OF TREND TRAPS

Products for the home follow a similar trend flow as the one for fashion. Trends tend to start in high-end furniture shows, glossy magazines, and projects where consumers and their design squad take more chances and have the real estate gumption to do something more daring. These trends, once thought exotic, get mass-produced by anyone selling anything for the home. This is why I can buy an ikat-printed dishtowel at my local supermarket. Buying like a designer means you are intimately in tune with what's available, but not swayed by popularity. Don't worry about trends.

Keep the focus on what pleases you. Do your own curating as opposed to following others. Has something you really want been in magazines lately? Is it considered hot or trendy by someone in design media? Then you're probably going to pay for that. Is the item you've got your eye on appearing in catalogs that show up on your doorstep weekly? Part of the price tag comes from all that mail. Branding is costly and accounts for part of the cost too. If you do fall in love with something trendy, know that it's probably available from about fifteen different sources. Don't buy it from the first place you see it. This is one of the best parts of online sourcing for the home: do a search for your desired item and see everyone's version and the range of price points. Ask yourself if you're buying this to be "on trend," one of my least favorite phrases in the English language. It makes it sound like you're on a train going in the right direction, with everyone else who bought the same on-trend item. Instead of being on trend, stay on point with your own desires and the building of your own aesthetic, something wholly independent of what anyone else is doing.

For those of you who've never worked with a professional designer or decorator, this is how it goes. After you meet with the designer to discuss your ideas (during which they hopefully listen attentively) he or she will create a visual aid of sorts—a presentation board to indicate what they'd like to do for your space. Sometimes, this will start as a concept board, or just a flavor of what they envision. More often, for smaller residential projects what you see first is a collage of the primary elements suggested for your room. Presentation boards include all sorts of swatches for paint, flooring, draperies, and upholstery, in addition to small images of furniture and perhaps samples of other details such as hardware. The board may also include an initial sketch or floor plan of the space.

As a contrast, most home owners I know keep swatches floating around in their purse or kitchen drawer, or in a paper envelope. They rarely enjoy the enormous benefit of seeing all their choices arranged on the same sheet of paper. Why not do this for yourself? Although it's used as a presentation tool for clients, this concept of arranging choices together on paper is enormously helpful for the process of composing a room. The room and all its colors and textures come alive on paper first—then you can tell if things aren't jiving.

If you have a room you are working on, find yourself either a clean two-page spread in your Home Book or a separate, large piece of paper, ideally poster board or something stiff. (You may glue tile to it.)

1. The first thing that goes on the page is a floor plan of the room, with measurements.

2. Next, add any givens that are staying put—existing hardwood floors or built-ins or even furniture—anything you're working around. Use a small photo or swatch if you have one or find a photo online that's a good match for each item that's staying. You now have your home base.

3. Hopefully you can find a picture or something that represents the kernel of the room, which we discussed earlier.

4. As you decide what you need for the space, which will flow from that initial kernel, paste your selections on to your board.

Art is the only way to run away without leaving home.

—TWYLA THARP

36

COLLECTING ART IS
NOT JUST FOR COLLECTORS

Find art for your home throughout your life.

Too often we're led to buy matchy-matchy art so that everything can be cohesive, as opposed to buying or using art we are truly connected to. The system of decorating and making everything match becomes the master, trumping what you really like, what speaks to you, and what expresses your beliefs. "This orange artwork works with my couch." But do you like it? "It's OK, but it really pops against my blue walls." This is not how you choose artwork. This is how you follow a formula for a room that works visually but not emotionally or spiritually. This is the recipe for a pretty room with no soul.

In high-end interior design magazines, art collectors are given the freedom to showcase art that does not jive with the system mentioned above. These home owners are invited, even celebrated, for using art that *doesn't* go with the rest of the room, presumably because the art is expensive or rare. Although I applaud the use of art not so much within the context of the room, but *regardless* of the context of the room, I reject the notion that you can only do this if the art is really valuable.

The important consideration for art is whether you want to be around it and what feelings it evokes in you. Choose pieces that stir you immediately. Forget about what others think, what goes with it, or its monetary value. Don't be overly concerned about color—pay more attention to texture and shapes and the subject. What connections can you make between the art and your room, aside from color? Color is too limiting and says no to art that might work nicely for reasons other than that it matches the couch.

I have paintings my husband gave me before we had things like swim lessons and babysitters to pay for. They remind me of that time, and I love the art. The feelings are fused. I also have works from artists I've known. And I have pieces I love for no good reason. I just enjoy looking at them. Some are cheap, perhaps cheaply framed, and I adore them all the same. The most enjoyable way to buy art is to buy it for love, without knowing whether you have a place for it or how it will work in your house. You've heard the expression "Leap and the net will appear"? Do you love that piece of art? Then a spot will appear.

Our sons' preschool teacher and family friend, Lizzie Flavin, a woman who loves the artful home she's in, gave me a tour of the paintings in her cozy-yet-dashing library. I remember her telling me about these paintings with a twinkle in her eye: "This is a painting of the village where I grew up in England. This was painted by my cousin. This was a painting of my mother's village in England. This was bought in Georgetown where I met my husband. I just love them all." She then pointed to the bookshelf full of books written by authors she's known throughout her life, with equal exuberance. This kind of enthusiasm doesn't come from art bought to match the couch.

Choosing art is not about having some kind of idyllic bohemian lifestyle surrounded by fabulously creative people. This is about gathering as you go (perhaps a watercolor instead of another sweatshirt as a souvenir next time you're on a trip) and using what's meaningful on your walls. Lizzie's collection of pencil sketches, watercolors, prints, old maps, oil paintings, and framed pictures made sense with her white-and-blue library. The art didn't all match or have the same color scheme as the upholstery, but it was much more interesting that way, and collectively it all worked. Art says something, it has an emotional quality. If you're choosing art because it has a lot of beige in it or because it's 40 inches wide, chances are the feelings that come from the piece aren't what you intended.

I am working with a woman named Diane, who was really struggling to love her massive two-story family room space. She kept trying oversized works of art and mirrors—giant, contemporary, Vegas-like pieces that she didn't like but thought the room "needed" because of its scale. I found a framed watercolor of her alma mater in her basement. The look on Diane's face when I held it up told me all I needed to know. If you gush and smile warmly when you see a framed piece of art, it needs to go up on your wall. Diane's watercolor was not terribly big, but we made it the centerpiece and were able to use other large elements to offset the size of the room. We pulled all the colors of the room from that piece, and I don't know what happened on that campus years ago, but it was something good—having that piece on her mantel makes Diane almost laugh out loud every time she walks by.

Art for the house can include professional paintings, drawings, and prints, but don't limit yourself to these, especially if you can't afford professional art. It can also include your own work, framed photographs, decorative plates and ceramics, your child's work, tapestries, vintage papers or ephemera (like album covers or old sewing patterns, maps, old postcards), objects from nature, posters, silhouettes, metalwork, collections, and more.

Buy art from artists. It doesn't need to be expensive or exclusive, but know something about the creator or the story of your art. A home full of art and artists' stories bubbles with authenticity and personality. If there is something you want but can't afford, wait—but don't wait with white walls. Find affordable art and things you like to look at and use them, or make your own. What works is up to you; there are no art police who'll come to your home and tell you that you're wrong. Have faith in yourself and your response to what you like. What counts is the feeling, so pay attention! No one else can know what works for your heart.

Do you have a work of art you really love? Perhaps there is a story behind it that makes you smile. Let this piece lead you in a room that needs a change. Especially if you're not using the artwork at the moment.

First, really look at your art. Take in the subject, colors, textures, and overall mood of the piece. Second, identify what you love about it. The subject? The colors? The expression? Third, pull a paint color from this piece. Lay your artwork on the floor in a relatively sunny spot in the room you're working on. Ideally, you'll have your own fan deck from the paint store of your choice. (They usually cost about $25.) Whatever you choose will be amplified in the artwork once you paint. Don't worry too much about matching exactly, but it's not a bad idea to steal a great paint color from a painting you love. It's one of my favorite tricks.

Last, think about what other qualities from this piece you can bring into the room. Geometric shapes? Latin culture? Whatever you love about the piece can be brought into the room somehow—through decorative objects, such as vases, bookends, lamps, flowers, and table linens—and fill many of the blanks for a tough space. Pull your answers from that art you already love. As that old tomato sauce commercial used to say, "It's in there!"

There is one fundamental
fact about lighting:
Where there is no light,
there is no beauty.

—BILLY BALDWIN

37

LET THERE BE LIGHT

Consider the three basic lighting needs for every room.

In Esther Sternberg's inspiring and intriguing book, *Healing Spaces: The Science of Place and Well-Being*, she explores the connection between architecture and health. The first time this was demonstrated was in an early 1980s study of hospital patients, half of whom were in rooms without a window and half of whom had a room with a window and a view of the outside world. Those in the room with a view healed faster and left the hospital sooner. The mechanics of a window's impact on the healing process are not understood, although they continue to be studied. This is probably not a huge shock to anyone. Who would want a bedroom, or any room, without a window? We are instinctively drawn to light.

Humans need light and visual access to the outdoors to live well. Light is precious, no matter where or how you live. Light in a house changes everything—the goal is not only to have light but to maximize and manage natural light, integrate the right kinds of artificial light, and make sure that both functional needs (chopping onions without losing a finger) and emotional needs (healing faster, managing emotions, seeing your partner's face) are all taken into account. Lighting your home is as important as any other design or furniture decision you can possibly make.

There are three types of artificial lighting you'll want to consider for each room in your house. The first is *task lighting*, which illuminates a specific work surface to enable you to do things like typing, chopping, diaper changing, and reading. The second is *ambient lighting*, which affects the color and mood of a room and is the hardest to master. A dimly lit room is quieter and more dramatic; it can also be more drab and depressing. A well-lit room is more lively and energized, but it can also be jarring and overly bright. The last type is *accent lighting*, which is used as a sort of finger pointing toward something worth showcasing in your home. Use accent lighting to highlight furniture, artwork, photography, a walkway, or an architectural feature. Ambient and accent lighting are personal choices, even physiological ones. My husband is very sensitive to bright natural light, I am not. He is often closing the blinds in our kitchen, while I am quick to open them. Whoever is cooking gets to decide.

It is not outlandish to consider three different lighting sources for nearly any sized room to reflect the needs of task, ambient, and accent lighting. Even in a bathroom, there are times when you need to see things up close, times when you need a dim light for a quick middle-of-the-night visit, and times when it makes sense to illuminate the room for use during the day. Three different circumstances call for three different lights. I find that lighting is most often overlooked in rooms where there is no task-lighting need per se. We overlook our complex lighting needs in bedrooms and living rooms. We choose lights for looks, and don't consider what we really need to see in the space.

LIGHTBULBS

Does your lightbulb affect how the colors look in your room? Yes, though this can be hard to control. There are two metrics regarding color and lightbulbs. The first is the color of the light itself, which is measured in Kelvins. There is a scale from warm to cool, which is not always demarcated on a box of bulbs. Some manufacturers prefer to print "warm" or "cool" on the package. The other consideration is how the bulb renders color. The color rendering index (CRI) speaks to this. Again, this is more often the domain of electrical contractors than consumers, but it's good to know when you're talking to an electrical contractor that you are looking for warm light (most of us are) but want to balance relative efficiency and service life. (They will love you for knowing even just a bit of this.)

Overlighting a space is barely possible, but overbrightening it is another story. You don't want to make a room brighter than is comfortable for your eyes or the ambience you're trying to create. Lots of recessed lights can make a space too bright, like being inside a big-box retailer store all the time. Dimmer switches give you maximum control and provide a range of choices for any kind of lighting.

My approach to lighting is to provide many different options, even in small rooms like the powder room. My living room has a fireplace, and when it's just my family and I, the fireplace and a table lamp suffice. However, I have three other light sources in that space if I have a party, or people are eating there, or I just feel like I need more light. There is something strange about sitting in a room with people who are not your intimates, if the room is a bit too dim.

Lighting design depends on trial and error. If you've ever worked in the theater, you know that lighting is an art, not a science. It must be manipulated based on what performer is standing where at what time and what mood is being expressed. In your home, think about the who, what, when, and where for each room when considering all the lighting needs you will have in each space.

YOUR TURN
LIGHTING QUIZ

If you are struggling with which lights to buy or where to install fixtures in your space, take this quiz.

1. *What tasks am I doing in this room? Will I need to see something up close?* Task lighting comes in many shapes and forms. There are lots of options (wall- or ceiling-mounted fixtures, ceiling or table lamps), and the operative question is, "Does the fixture direct light toward what I'm doing?"

2. *What mood am I creating in this room once the sun goes down?* Ambient lighting is typically uplighting, or lighting that fills the room with diffuse light. You need not buy all new fixtures if you

are unhappy with the lighting in your space. Consider installing or having a dimmer installed so you can manage the amount of light you get from your fixtures. Consider the range of lightbulbs—compact fluorescents (CFLs) and light-emitting diode (LED) bulbs—with assorted wattages that offer different colors and intensities.

3. *What might I like to accent in this space?* Perhaps you want to accent a work of art or sculpture. But you may also wish to highlight a particular texture in your home, such as wallpaper or stucco or tapestry, at night, which creates a beautiful effect. This can be done with wall sconces. Accent lighting doesn't serve much purpose other than to insert light for beauty's sake. Perhaps there is a beautiful fixture that doesn't give off much light but is very pleasant to look at when it's on—in effect, the accent light is the accent. This is great as long as your functional bases are already covered.

When the sun is shining
I can do anything; no
mountain is too high, no
trouble too difficult to overcome.

—WILMA RUDOLPH

38

DRESSING YOUR WINDOWS
FOR ALL OCCASIONS

Pick smart window treatments,
and exploit and manage natural light
for maximum benefit.

Right after "How do I pick a paint color?" the most popular
question with home owners is "What window treatment should I
choose?" Many are stymied, perhaps because there are so many
choices, but also because window treatments can be complicated
to understand, let alone install, and they can be very expensive. In
most cases, they are machines, some simpler than others, devised
to manage natural light coming into your house.

Typically, there are multiple functions we ask window
treatments to perform. In a bedroom, for instance, windows are
sometimes asked to flood the space with light and breeze, but other
times they must shut out any light and cold air whatsoever. Consider
first what you need your windows and their coverings to do. Second,
consider the proportion of the window to the room. If the room is
small and limited in floor space, a lower-volume window treatment
is better (a Roman shade versus full draperies). Third, consider what
part the window will play in the aesthetics of the room. Windows
and their treatments can be features of a space, commanding
attention with statement fabrics and tall heights, or they can take a

backseat with minimalist covering and allow the rest of the room, or even the view outside, to be the focus.

FUNCTION

Consider the level of privacy you need your window treatments to give you. If you need privacy all the time because it's a bathroom window or you just prefer that no one sees in, consider what portion of the window needs to be covered and what should cover the bottom half, if applicable. Consider sheer fabrics or shades that allow light to come in while keeping prying eyes out. If you need privacy some of the time, as is the case with a bedroom or family room, then choose one of the options I've already mentioned, blinds that can shut out all light and view, or shutters that can also be opened or closed. If you have different needs at different times of the day or year, make sure the mechanism to open and close the treatment is easy to use and well made. Buy a higher quality mechanism if you are going to use it every day. This is the case if you are managing light that may be too bright during some part of the day but welcome at other times.

Window treatments function to filter light. If you need the room to be completely dark (I can't sleep with any light in the room), use room-darkening devices. There are lots of choices here. Presuming you don't want to shut out the light all day, choose a good-quality mechanism for a standard roller shade or an opaque drape that can close completely. Room-darkening, or blackout curtains, may also have heat-sealing properties that control the chill from drafty windows as well. One of my favorite sources for window treatments, specifically room-darkening roll shades, is Country Curtains, a family-owned business operating out of Massachusetts, with great customer service.

SCALE

I live in a relatively small house. For most of my house, I simply don't have the room for drapes to the floor, which need plenty of room to fall and look best when they are full. If you don't have the space for this, a treatment that is tailored to the window is probably better, such as a shade or blinds. To mimic the elongating effect of hanging curtains high on the wall, consider a cornice hung above the window but covering the very top portion, to make the window look taller.

COLOR AND TEXTURE

Certainly this is the most fun, as there are few things as room-changing as good window treatments. Consider what is in the rest of the room and how much attention you'd like the window to command. It's perfectly all right to choose window treatments that "go away," or seem to disappear into the wall. Perhaps they are the same color as the wall. Maybe they are simple and understated, which makes sense if the focus is the view or the rest of the elements in the room. A layered window treatment—such as a drape over a roman shade, a cornice over a solar shade, or dummy panels (drapes that don't close and are mounted on the outer edges of the window) along with shutters—are options that offer aesthetic value and shaping. It's nice to have contrast even on the windows, such as the soft fabrics and hard edges of a cornice, smooth fabric on curtains alongside a woven shade, and so on.

Think about what color and texture would make you happy with the rest of what you have in that room. Think about your seasons. Dark, heavy fabrics may feel leaden and dreary in summer. Lighter linens may feel too airy in winter. Also, keep in mind that the light that comes from the window, assuming it's welcome at least part of the day, is like gold. Sunlight floods your home with warmth and boosts moods. Make sure that when the window is open, it's open as much as possible, meaning you can see as much of the window as possible unencumbered. Sheers or light-filtering shades can do the job of protecting interior furnishings from fading or otherwise degrading over time from the sun's ultraviolet rays. This is an inexpensive alternative to replacing your windows with high-performance glass or installing films onto the glass.

If you are using curtains or drapes, the hardware is as important as the fabric. Choose carefully and pick something you'll enjoy looking at, presuming you'll see at least part of it on the window. Most drapery hardware is too thin or fragile. The bigger the window, the wider and heftier you want the rod or finials or hardware apparatus to be—not just because it'll be carrying more weight but because proportionately, a larger window needs a more significant structure to be balanced.

The View Outside

What does it look like from the front yard? When you're outside the house, you're looking at the underside of your window treatments. If the appearance of your window treatments is visible from your front lawn, consider layering any soft fabric drapes with blinds, shades, or plantation shutters, which give a uniform shape and texture across multiple rooms.

When you are shopping for window treatments, it helps to have all of your measurements handy. This means the measurements for the length and width of the window itself, inside the window trim, if you have it. Measure the distance from the bottom of the window (on the inside of the trim) to the floor as well. Measure the distance from the ceiling to the floor. Measure the distance from the top of the window trim to the ceiling. Measure the width of your window trim. Instead of carrying around a bunch of notes with numbers scribbled on them, save yourself the trouble of having to measure again and again and make a simple window treatment diagram. Or go one better and draw an elevation view of the wall where the windows exist. This means you'll draw a rectangular box to show the entire wall, draw a box to show where the window is on the wall, and then pencil in all of your measurements.

Carrying this, as well as a photo, with you when you're shopping at the store or online will also help you visualize the window fully dressed.

The cruel irony of housework: people only notice when you don't do it.

—DANIELLE RAINE,
HOUSEWORK BLUES:
A SURVIVAL GUIDE

39

EVERYTHING IN ITS PRETTY PLACE

Be choosy as you organize and
find materials for containers that
suit your space.

Full disclosure—I am disorganized. I exercise tremendous discipline (against my true nature and not all the time) to do the daily pruning required to keep a household organized. I am scatterbrained and overly sentimental, and I hang on to things way too long with good intentions totally disconnected from reality. There is probably nothing worse than a dreamer/pack rat to a professional organizer. My only hope is to make the mess look good. I'm more willing to be part of a system of organization that I like to look at; I'm more inclined to use the pretty bins I chose or to put stuff away in a closet that is just as good-looking as the room. Making it pretty is my hook. This could go in the "fake it 'til you make it" category, because just having pretty bins doesn't mean you're organized. However, it is the first step. It's also a way to connect our aesthetic with the random, disparate, abundant stuff around us that sometimes seems to want to swallow us whole.

My sister-in-law Julie taught me the pretty bin trick. Julie has impeccable taste and a gorgeous house, but this tip is meaningful even if your house is just starting down the road toward gorgeous, so don't be intimidated. All you need to know is what you like. The concept is to buy an interesting, attractive container for everything that needs to be contained. "Pretty containers for everything," Julie said to me one day, as I watched her dump Barbie shoes and Elmo books into a gorgeous, oversized tufted ottoman that opened, well before gorgeous, tufted storage ottomans were cool. One of the aesthetic hardships with having children is their abundance of stuff. Most of it is not in line with the story I'm telling in my living room of nature, calm, and dreamy water-based vacations.

KID STUFF—NOT KID CONTAINERS

Children's retailers and baby stores would very much like to sell you a toy chest or a series of brightly colored baskets for toys, which elves will presumably come and fill with your kids' detritus after you go to sleep. These may be ideal for children's spaces, but what about when the children are playing in the adult spaces? Legos are part of my daily life, but they are not necessarily invited guests in my living room. My friend Ellen, who lived in Asia for six years, had a Lego table made several years ago. It's some table— sophisticated and elegant, with traditional Chinese curvature and detail in the legs, lacquered in black. Only when the two top panels slide open are the Legos revealed in a secret compartment painted red. Ellen can keep the Lego building supplies of her four children handy, within the elegance of a room created by people who've crisscrossed Asia in their travels.

Give yourself the gift of something you like looking at as a repository for toys or pet stuff in each room of your house. Choose bins for toys to be sorted, toys to give away, toys that need new batteries, Bob's toys, Betty's toys, Baby's toys, and so on. They don't all have to be the same, or they can all be identical with interesting name tags or monograms. It doesn't matter. Just make sure you like to look at them and can move them around as needed.

A NOTE ABOUT CLOSETS AND CABINETS

You may think my container advice only applies to things outside of closed doors, but that's not true. Things that are in the room proper are more visible, but you deserve to look at interesting containers wherever they are. It's less frequent but no less entertaining to open the door to a closet and be delighted. Painting the inside of a closet can also make your storage space more surprising and pretty. Use a color you're dying to try. Or practice putting up wallpaper. Do something so that every time you open a closet, it's like a cheery little wink all for you. Per my opening caveat, I certainly don't have the last word on closet organization, but making a closet work is a lot about grouping things according to how they're used, putting them together in the right-sized containers or drawers, and keeping them all that way. Whether you use elegant rattan boxes, hot pink Lucite bins, or canvas beach bags, use what you like, even when no one else gets to see.

THINK OUTSIDE THE BIN

Consider the Container Store, of course, but also think about anything that holds other things as an option for your pretty container. A salad bowl might be more interesting and more functional than a basket for storing your keys. A mail bin may be ideal for sunscreen in the summertime. A sturdy beach tote may be just the memory-laden ticket for hats and gloves in the winter. It doesn't need to be expensive, you just need to like it. Look at baskets, boxes, old trunks, even interesting suitcases. It seems like my dear friends Brad and Jill Olander are always buying something interesting and smart, something that no one else has but probably should. The latest is a set of handmade leather suitcases, which are breathtakingly beautiful. They are part Great Gatsby, part Indiana

Jones, and it would be a sin to stow them unseen. Jill says, "Since we really have nowhere else to store them, we keep them on top of our armoire in our living room. They are so gorgeous, and we keep guest linens inside." While the luggage may be pricey, it serves three purposes as something pretty to look at, a reminder of Brad and Jill's trips to Napa together, and a place for extra sheets—brilliant.

You can't be organized without good containers and lots of them. But you also need discipline; a strategy for getting rid of stuff; and a system for the inflow and outflow of toys, clothing, food, trash, personal items, and so on. For now, don't worry if you don't have all that. (I don't either.) Just start with pretty containers. They go a long way.

YOUR TURN
MAKE YOUR BIGGEST PROBLEM PRETTY

What is your biggest mess? What items are hardest for you to keep organized? Do you struggle with toys? Beauty products? Mail? Whatever it is, treat yourself to something beautiful that will contain the problem in some way. It doesn't need to hold everything or solve the problem completely, but if your stuff is out and creating an eyesore, you have to fight back. Focus on buying one pretty container (a bowl, bin, basket, box, or suitcase) that will house some or all of the unsightly things. The only rule is to make sure you love the container and are excited to use it.

40

LESS IS MORE

*Be selective about what you love,
and find the sweet spot between not
enough and too much of a good thing.*

"Enough" is a concept that eludes me in almost every part of daily life. I like almost anything in big quantities, yet I've learned that there's beauty and joy in fewer things that mean more to me. The less time I take to think about a room, the more stuff I use in that space. When I spend more time considering what I really enjoy—what's meaningful and what really works—the number of things I use gets much smaller. It's not minimalism that I'm after, it's the paring down of things to get to the good stuff, the clearing out of things that don't offer me what I'm looking for—big visual pleasure, inspiration, or reminders of great things in my life.

You can reduce some of the best creative advice down to a well-worn quote, applicable to all sorts of creative endeavors: "Edit, edit, edit." It's consistent with everything we've been working on. It means being choosy and remembering that if you have too many things to look at in any room, everything gets watered down. If you keep the focus on what you love and what you're connected to, what's connected to the space, and what feels right to you, you won't have too much, nor will you have an empty space.

TOO MUCH FURNITURE

Most people overfurnish. Avoid this mistake, which hinders the use of the room and makes it feel tighter and less comfortable. It happens when you don't think through the function of a room and when you hold on to stuff you don't love. As I've said already, start by imagining the function of the room. Who needs to sit? Will they want a drink here? Where will they put it? Whoever sits there may want to put their feet up, where will they do that? Will they be reading? What will the source of reading light be? I encourage you to think through these questions as opposed to saying, "I need a couch, a coffee table, and a chair," without thinking about who will be using the pieces and how. Certainly there are unknowns when we have guests or parties. Do you entertain often? Do you have a big family? Is it primarily you and your immediate family enjoying the space? Design for your immediate family and plan for events when they come, as opposed to having extra fixed pieces for all the days they will go unused.

Another pitfall is placing furniture too far apart. If you can't have a conversation with someone sitting on each piece of furniture in a particular seating area without yelling, then your furniture is too far apart. Bring it closer; don't spread it out just because you have a big space. Create two distinct usable areas if you have an extra-large living room. Rather than thinking about what you're *supposed* to do, or even what the space dictates, see what you like. Maybe it feels better to have your couch in the middle of the room if it means you can create a good cluster for conversation and socializing. Maybe you only use a third of your vast living room so you can cluster the furniture appropriately—that's much better than spreading all the seating so far out it's as if each person would have to yell to have a conversation with someone in the opposite chair or couch. If you are an overfurnisher, put the underused pieces in storage for now. Live without them for a few days or weeks. How does the space feel? Does it open up? Does it bother you to have the space unoccupied? Trust your own feeling about the space and what works for social activities, as opposed to some sort of rule you read in a magazine or heard from your mother-in-law. A good concept to think about is the campfire. We haven't evolved all that much since the days when families or friends would gather around a fire for warmth and companionship. The campfire has been replaced by a coffee table, and sometimes a television, but the goal of intimacy and connection remains.

> *One cannot collect all the beautiful shells on the beach. One can collect only a few, and they are more beautiful if they are few.*
>
> **—ANNE MORROW LINDBERGH**

TOO MUCH PRETTY

Perhaps you have overaccessorized. When I was working on HGTV, we had a stylist named Amy Salinger, who is very blunt. She took accessories seriously—not just the placement of accessories but the balance of them on the person. Different pieces accentuate or call attention to different parts of your body. Amy styled me throughout my first pregnancy; there was a lot of playing up and away from my enormous belly. Each accessory had a job. Think of the accessories for your home the same way. They each have a purpose and a beauty, each of them draws the eye in a specific way. Too much of something, even pretty things, doesn't work. If it isn't serving a purpose or isn't simply fabulous on its own, let it go. Allow for space between your things to allow the eye to take more in.

It's refreshing to rearrange the furniture and arrange things on shelves and mantels when trying to nail "the interestingly composed vignette of things." Don't be surprised if it takes you a long time— maybe months or even years to get a certain surface right in terms of accessories. Make sure you enjoy looking at what's there and are not just keeping stuff out because you have it. This is a good project for your creative counsel. My grandmother was always refreshing her house with different things to look at. It seemed like she had a wreath for each month of the year. Her home always looked different, and that's what made it great. From time to time, you may also change your mind on what you want to see out. I have found that our house moods can change: during some seasons, we may enjoy having a lot to look at; in others, we enjoy a cleaner, more blank space.

YOUR TURN
TABLETOP REBOOT

Do you think you may have too many decorative items in your house? Or maybe a certain spot just doesn't look right. Clean off a few surfaces. Take things off a shelf and leave it empty, clear off the top of your dresser, bare your mantel. Live like this for a few days. Give all the surfaces a good cleaning, then bring things back slowly and selectively. You will most likely place them more mindfully. Give yourself permission to arrange things differently—or not to put anything back at all.

AFTERWORD

LETTING GO OF "DONE"

After so much work—thinking, vision-creating, list-making, tradesmen-hiring, DIY-ing, paying, redoing, analyzing, and cleaning—you likely have a great longing to be done. Change is expensive, whether you're paying with your money or your time. When will it all be done?

Never.

Your house may feel complete from time to time, and hopefully you will sometimes feel immensely confident that you don't need to undertake any new projects. But you are not done. Steaks get done; great houses get worked on forever. Homes don't get finished any more than we ourselves do. As soon as you get your home to that acceptable place, life intervenes. Maybe you lose a parent or get a job offer in Europe; maybe a tree falls on your house; maybe you go through menopause or have a first baby. And all those shiny spaces either get forcibly rearranged or they just don't feel right any longer.

I've found, through trial and error and watching my own and other people's homes, that the best way to love your house is to create it and mold it over many years—in fact, throughout your lifetime. The itch to have something done, to check off the proverbial boxes, to complete something unfinished is human, but it's not going to lead you to love. Being done means we know everything we need, desire, and feel comforted by right now. It means our home reflects us completely, both aesthetically and in terms of what we need it to do for us. This is a tall order, and it takes time. We, ourselves, are never really "done" enough for this to be possible.

No matter how difficult it is to be in process, I've seen so much good come of waiting and curating my home with life's artifacts and pieces of my journey, as opposed to what works right now or what will suffice so I can be done. Recently, my sons started putting stuff from their time outside into the big wooden bowl I have on top of the console in my foyer—tree bark, acorns, fool's gold, bugs in jars. They've started hanging things on the big chunky frames on the wall above—beaded necklaces, a shark's tooth on a string, and artwork. Their contributions make the whole wall work better than it did before when it was neat and tidy and lacking the earthiness that only bugs in jars can bring. The colors and textures work quite magically, and I like that my sons were complicit in my obsessive accessorizing. The console is always being undone, changed up, and added to. This is far more perfect than being done.

See your home as a project, an experiment, a laboratory, an ongoing art installation. What makes your home is not just how it looks today; it is all you hope it will become over time and the joy of knowing how far it's come. More love comes from a house that's always keeping up with you, always evolving and staying fresh. If you don't love your house today, it doesn't have enough of you in it. What small piece of you can you add today? We often associate big change with house love, but it's often a more subtle process of adding, deleting, tinkering, and creating day by day, over time.

Seeing your house as a laboratory is much more enjoyable than seeing it as something on your to-do list. I had a health scare about a year before I wrote this book. I found a prayer in a book I was reading that changed my perspective and filled me with faith. That prayer is now featured on the wall at the top of my stairs in letters that are five inches tall, so I can look at it each and every day as I climb the stairs and brace myself for our bedtime rituals. Each time I reread that prayer on my wall, I think of the first time I read it. It is the perfect jolt of hope each and every night, a perfect reminder of the grace I was given during that challenging time. Life provided the best art for my hallway. I'm so happy I didn't just hang stuff there so I could be done.

Do this work. Stay true to yourself. Make it thoughtful. That's my prayer for you. Not because I don't want you to go out and buy the first pretty thing you see but because I know the magic that comes from a house created over time *through* life. Best of luck to you and your house on this journey—I know you'll be very happy together!

As you move toward a dream [house], the dream [house] moves toward you.

—JULIA CAMERON

ACKNOWLEDGMENTS

I used to think it was trite to say, "This book/movie/project would not have been possible without the following individuals," but that is completely true in my case. This book and I benefited from a supportive ecosystem of people who've inspired, encouraged, taught, prodded, whipped, loved, occasionally left alone, and often prayed for me. The idea for this book came directly from HGTV viewers and their e-mails—the thousands of people who deeply wanted more from their homes and thought enough of this wish, and me, to ask for my help. I am duly grateful to all the friends and clients in my current community in Kensington, Maryland, in Summit, New Jersey, and in and around New York City who invited me into their homes and the most intimate spaces of their lives. If you want or have wanted your house to be better with all your heart, you are the reason for this book and many of you are mentioned in it!

I am eternally grateful to my dear friend Paula Atkinson, who introduced me to *The Artist's Way* by Julia Cameron and, by extension, life outside panty hose and straight lines. Thank you for always knowing the right thing to say to an artist who needs her cup filled. I am profoundly grateful to Joelle Delbourgo, my literary agent, who believed in this project from the beginning and stuck with it like glue—and encouraged me to do the same. I could not have written this book without my editor at Roost Books, Jenn Urban-Brown, who simply made the book better and whose patience with me and trust in this project have felt limitless, though I'm certain I have tested them.

I am grateful to my sisters-in-law, Teresa, Cecilia, and Julie, who have shown me the art of family life and how beautiful homes with happy children can be. Through you, I have learned that great beauty at home must not happen despite children but because of them.

My creative career would not have existed were it not for my parents, who taught me confidence and instilled the kind of guts you must have to pursue a career in both television and writing. Thanks to my father-in-law, Frank, not only for teaching my husband, Francis, how to care for a house as a boy but for inspiring him to be the kind of man who *enjoys* fixing, repairing, and perpetually improving a house. Francis, thank you for saying yes to so many different ideas of mine in so many different houses (many of which were not good) and for enjoying the beautiful art of home-building as much I do. I love it when my dreamy idealism meets your practical smarts (and ample tool arsenal), and the result is another thing that makes our house better. I love you, thank you for helping me make this happen. Thank you to my sons, Xavier, Luke, and Nicholas, and my daughter, Teresa, for being the most beautiful and precious things in our home, for teaching me the value of Mr. Clean Magic Eraser, and for breaking lots of things I never really liked anyway. Life is better with you in it.

INDEX